LIBRARY
AND
INFORMATION TECHNOLOGY

LIBRARY
AND
INFORMATION TECHNOLOGY

By

Dr. P.V. Subba Rao

M.A., M.L., I.Sc.

Assistant Librarian

Acharya Nagarjuna University

Nagarjuna Nagar–522 510

SONALI PUBLICATIONS

NEW DELHI-110002

Edition **2017**
ISBN 81-88836-86-9

Published by
SONALI PUBLICATIONS
4228/1, Ansari Road,
New Delhi-110 002 (India)
Phone: 23266109, 23279245 • Fax: 91-11-23253475

Printed at:
Amit Enterprises, Delhi

PREFACE

The volume of information was not as large as it is today, and the libraries were in a position to organize the information materials through manual operation. But since the Second World War there has been a tremendous output of information, which has been usually referred to as information explosion. The materials of information in both print and non-print media—manuscripts, books, journals, reports, films, discs, tapes (i.e. a variety of information packages) — continue to be produced and used in greater and greater quantities. This vast amount of information has to be processed, stored and retrieved whenever required. The very complexity and magnitude of the problem makes it an impossible task to process by manual method. Library and information scientists are increasingly being compelled to take the help of semiautomatic and automatic machines for information handling.

The revolutionary developments in information technology have two impacts. Firstly, as more and more information is readily available in machine-readable form, there has been a fundamental shift in the concerns of the information profession from 'more information' to 'accurate, up-to-date and timely information'. Secondly, as computers are used increasingly for provision of information, librarians and other information professionals must familiarize themselves with the latest technological development in this field.

Libraries have traditionally been considered as store houses of various kinds of macro-documents, shelved in a linear, hierarchical, apparently useful, but precoordinated and prearranged sequence.

CONTENTS

1

Introduction to Computer

Definition of Computer

1. According to Chambers Dictionary of Science and Technology, "Computer is any mechanical, electric or electronic apparatus; or assembly which performs calculations, simple or including integration and differentiation or simultaneous equations."
2. McGraw-Hill Concise Ency. of Science and Technology defines computer as "A device that receives, processes and resent information".

When we apply to library and information centers whatever data regarding Library Administration, Cataloguing, Classification, Circulation, Readers Services etc. received and processed internally with machine language we gather the information from the computer.

In order to gain a better perspective of the theory and practice of Computer, it is necessary in this context to get a gums of the history of Computer.

History of Computers

The computer existing at present has come from ABACUS in this world. The ABACUS is a "computing instrument, consisting of beads (counter) strung on wires mounted in a frame". It is an extremely ancient device that has been in use for thousands of years in various firms, and is still commonly used in China, Japan and other parts of the middle east. Its exact date is unknown when came to society in this world but in the Greek Historian Herodotus period might have come that is between 485-425 BC.

In 1693 another great German Mathematician, and Philosopher Mr. G.W. Leibritz has extended the idea of Pascal that is "to design a desk calculator with multiply and device". In 1812 Cambridge University Mathematics Professor Mr. Charles Babbage has developed "a machine which would automatically calculated trigonometric and logarithmic tables. Therefore, it was used by difference method of ccmputation". Simultaneously another calculator was searched that was called "Analytical engine". This calculator has two distinct parts "a store to hold data until they were to act as operands and mill to process the data. Answers were to be returned to the store for future reference".

During 1890 an employee of the Census Bureau of United States Mr. Herman Hollerith has used "to store digital information by presence or absence of a series of holes on the card: Once information is stored in this form, machine will help in huge/very large task of enumeration inherent in the taking of a census.

Simultaneously he formed the tabulating machine compulsory which after a number of mergers and name changes; became in 1924 the International Business Machines-Corporation (IBM), the world's biggest computer company and the world leader in the field.

In 1937 Mr. Howard Aiken who was an employee of Harvard University ultimately" designed an electromechanical calculator to that machine, called "Automatic sequence controlled calculator" Mark I, which prepared mathematical tables by performing automatically a set of sequence of arithmetic operations:

The Electronic Digital Computer

The Moore School of Engineering of the University of Pennsylvania employee Mr. J. Presper Eckert and John W. Mauchly used electronic components instead of mechanical relays, for Computer. This machine was called "Electronic Numerical Integrator and Calculator" (ENIAC). This giant machine weighed 30 tons, had 18,000 vacuum tubes, 70,000 resisters,10,000 capacitor and 6,000 switches and it occupied a large zoom.

The Universities and Research laboratories have begun, research on ENIAC and find out another computer known as

Electronic Discrete Variable Automatic Computer (EDVAC), which is basically different from ENIAC in two ways; (a) the use of binary, numbers and (b) the internal storage of instructions: written in digital form.

The first installation of an electronic digital computer for business applications was made at the General Electronic Appliance Park in Louisrille Kentuoky.

Computer Generations

The Computer may be classified in five generations:

1. ***First Generation Computers:*** In this generation, computers were based on "Vacuum Tubes". This type of computer weighed 30 tons, had 18,000 vacuum tubes, 70,000 resistors,10,000 capacitor and 6,000 switches and it occupied a large room. At present this type of computers are not found in the society, though these may be seen in the computer museums.
2. ***Second Generation Computers:*** In this generation, Computers were based on "solid state discrete transistor circuits". These are very bulky, low and absolute.
3. ***Third Generation Computers:*** In this Generation, the computers were of integrated circuits-primarily small scale integrated (SSI) circuits (less than ten gates or switches per chip). Compared to the present day computers, these computes are treated as bulky, slow and absolute.
4. ***Fourth Generation Computers:*** Computers presently available in the society include this category. Here medium scale integrated (MSI) Circuits (less than 100 gates per chips) large scale integrated (LSI) circuits (less than 1000 gates per chips) and very large scale integrated (VLSI) chips are used to build the computer system. These computers are very fast, small in size and are available at reasonable cost from manufacturers. The speed at which these ranges of computers are working can be stated interiors of executing millions of instructions per second. Three to six million instructions per second (MIPS) are common.
5. ***5th Generation Computers:*** In this generation we shall see which type of computers ,would come to society. Though the

heart of the fifth generation computers do comprise of LSI and VLSI chips, the style in which it operates will be far from the present-day fourth generation computers. I think the fifth generation computers do possess an element of "intelligence".

Types of Computers and their Purposes

There are three types of computers:

1. Analogue computer
2. Digital computer
3. Hybrid computer

However emphasis has been laid only on two of them .'

Analogue Computer: There are various definitions but here a few of them are explained.

1. A Analogue computer as, "A computer or computational device in which the problem variables are represented as continuous, varying physical quantities".
2. Analog Computer is a machine which operates with continuously varying amplitudes as contrasted with digital computer".

Purpose Analog Computer

There are two types of analog computer such as:

1. General purpose
2. Specific purpose

General Purpose: It is designed to solve many problems, given by the programmer, permitting development of different simulated models as needed.

Specific Purpose: Computer has a fixed programme with a few or no permitted adjustment. It is generally built into or appended to the physical system it serves.

This type of computer measures a quantity (just) like a voltameter). It performs a number of mathematical operations for solving an' equation and plots the output data on a graph. An analogue computer, like a slide rule with simplier and more direct than a digital computer.

For instance you might have seen the thermometer which records various mercury levels which based on changes in the temperature. When temperature rises, the mercury Level rises and when temperature falls, so does the mercury level. That is changes in temperature are shown by analogues or like changes in the level of mercury in the thermometer.

Analogue computers translate various physical conditions such as flow, pressures, mechanical or electrical speeds, and angular positions into mechanical or electrical analogues.

Digital Computers

The Dictionary of Science and Technology shows that a digital computer is "one which performs simple calculations at high speed by impulses, related to digits in a code".

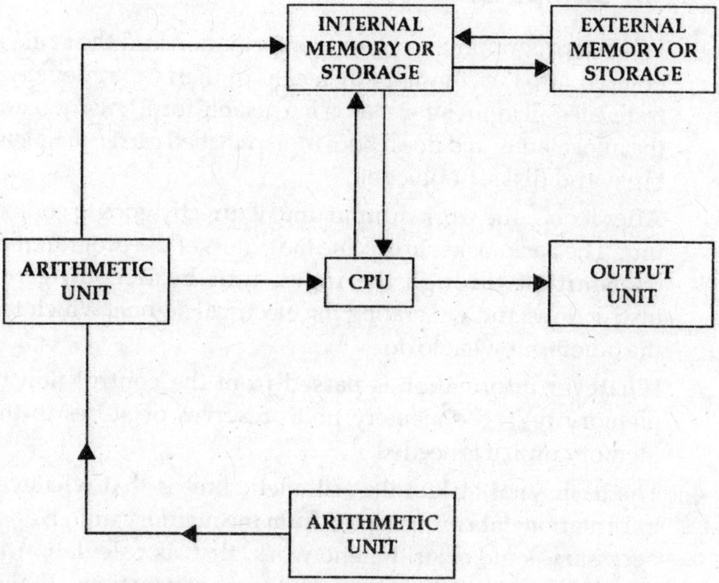

Figure 1.1. Architecture of Computer 4th Generation

The digital computer works rather than measures, works with digits but does not so in analogue computer. The computer (digital device) is designed to perform arithmetic operations on number supplied by an operator. The number may be 0 and 1, whereas the decimal system has ten digits – known as binary number system. These two binary digits or bits can be made to represent numbers, letters symbols, and codes by using various vertical and horizontal positing techniques.

All digital computers use the binary code; which has only two digits 0 and 1 represented electrically by a variety of two switching devices (states). In binary number system ON can be made to represent any 1 while OFF will represent a 0(zero).

In the computer binary system simple presence or absence of holes or magnetic spots on tapes provides the necessary instructions to computer to read, write, store, transmit and compute the solutions of great varieties of scientific, machine control, business and research problems, while computer will count, compare, store, retrieve and perform arithmetic functions multiplication, subtraction, additions etc.

Uses of Computer

1. When a programmer types any information and the same is entered into the computer by means of their input device, it translates all input information into usable form. Also it reads the information and does codes from punched cards, magnetic tapes and disks, floppies etc.
2. After it does the work in input unit, it directly goes to control unit. The basic task is to execute the orders of the programmer transmitted through the input, unit by decoding the instructions and generating the electrical signals which tell the other unit what to do.
3. Whatever information is passed from the control unit to memory unit, the memory unit preserves or stores in the memory until it is needed.
4. The basic vital task of the arithmetic unit is that whatever information data are accepted from the memory unit, it does necessary logic or arithmetic work, that, is calculation in accordance with stored programme of instructions. It also transfers the results to memory unit. All these work is going on under guidance and direction of control unit. The basic function of this unit is to workout multiplication, dividing, subtraction, adding etc. by logical process.
5. Whatever informations or data are accepted is duly processed by the memory and control units, where the data are represented by the electrical pulses. These signals from the control unit, and the output unit transmits them to peripheral equipment for use of digital or analogy signals.

Features of Computer

Whenever computer is installed at your institution/ organisation, check the necessary characteristics of computer as shown here:

1. Speed
2. Storage
3. Accuracy
4. Versatility
5. Automatic
6. Diligence

Computer Devices

There are two divisions of the computer such as:

1. Hardware
2. Software

But here emphasis has been laid on hardware.

Hardware

The hardware is nothing but body of the computer or physical units which are visible and tangible. It is a computer equipment.

Peripheral units + CPU = Computer.

1. Clock speed
2. Micro processor
3. ROM
4. RAM
5. Black and White Monitor
6. Floppy Drives
7. Hard Disc, Floppy
8. Keyboard
9. Printer
10. Ports
11. Switch mode power supply (SMS)
12. Stabilizer etc.

13. Real Time Clod (RTC) Battery, speaker etc. All these included in mother board.
14. Operating systems, MS-DOX, UNIXI/XENIX

The choice of the hardware selection is left to the Head of Institute/organisation. The Institute/organisation can purchase the hardware as required.

While installing the Computer configuration for various categories of Institutions or organisations, four important needs are to be considered:

1. Storage capacity
2. Processor speed
3. Software and
4. Net working capability

Hardware Requirement for Small Libraries

PC/XT

1. 8088 2 CPU (a) 8 or 10 MHz speed 640 KB main memory
2. 40 MB Winchester disk
3. 1 serial port and 1 parallel port
4. B/W monitor
5. MS-DOS operating system
6. CDS/ISIS or dBASE III Plus software
7. PC to PC communication software
8. 132 Col. MLW printer

Hardware Requirement for Medium Libraries

PC-XT/AT

1. 80386 based CPU
2. 4 M main memory
3. 160 MB Winchester disk
4. Serial and parallel ports
5. B/W monitor
6. 132 Col. MLW Printer
7. UNIX/XENIX Operating systems

8. CDS/ISIS software with application software to mother institution/organisation (Library and Information Centres) or dBASE III Plus programme.

Definition of Software

The computer programmes and designs of files to make the hardware perform the desired functions. It is a programme which uses the hardware to produce results. It represents the programme.

The computer software for library and information centre refers to computer programme in these words: "The Computer programme is a set of instructions composed for solving a given problem by computer", Mr. D.B. Patil said that - "The hardware and software of the computer are two faces of the same coin."

Operating System

It is a set of programmes, generally supplied by the computer manufacturer, which directly, controls the hardware and also coordinates the running of various applications. It consists of an operating system (also called the executive programme or master control programme) and other programmes and files are help to develop and maintain the applications, e.g. MS.DOS, UNIX/XENIX.

2

Computers in Libraries

Introduction

Libraries have traditionally been considered as store houses of various kinds of macro-documents, shelved in a linear, hierarchical, apparently useful, but precoordinated and prearranged sequence. Devoid of any publicity; the operations of the library were not known to the lay public. There was no glamour in the profession and the words library and Librarian with their unfortunate popular connotation, are stumbling blocks to establishing credibility with the lay public, other professionals such as engineers; technologists, medical practitioners, lawyers and the government. Exploding on the scene in the last three or four decades, the computers with an aura of glamour, myth and publicity attracted immediate attention. Handled, by sophisticated professionals with progressive outlook, the storage of any – data in computers is in a non-enumerative, random order with emphasis on post-coordination at the searching stage. Though the storage is in an arbitrary manner, the processing for any query received takes place. according to programmed instructions and the relevant information is quickly retrieved. There is also a built-in responsiveness to questions unforeseeable when the data is analysed at the input stage.

Development of Computers

The emergence of documentation towards the end of nineteenth century—a movement for the subject analysis and bibliographic organisation of periodical literature, though initially recognized as a legitimate library function—is a case in point. Provisions of physical access and content access to the materials in the library on a purely local basis became the main concern of the librarians as extension agents in public library promotion. The library profession failed to respond adequately to the needs of the professional research worker in his search for information reported in journal articles, reports and other non-book-based documents. The documentalists, borrowing the techniques and to a certain extent, the objectives of the earlier librarianship, ventured into the complexities of bibliographic organisation, developed and refined their own techniques for organisation and provision of services, and formed a separate organisation.

When data processing equipment and computers were utilized by non-librarians in the study of linguistics and incidentally in the machine extraction of key words or index terms from the natural language of the authors' publications, and in machine searching of full texts in small collections or prototype systems, the library professionals did not think high of these amateurish attempts in their citadel of well-proven, time-tested, systematic indexing and retrieval methods. The eminent librarians of traditional type of that era, wee only amused by these attempts and thought that the classification systems that had been/were being devised would stand the test of all time and withstand the onslaughts of machine-aided and automatic systems. But the non-librarians had gradually taken over completely the bibliographic activity relating to non-book materials. Moreover, in the 1960's and '70s, computers were not cost-effective either in storing complete documents/full texts or in application to library operations. The advent of microfilm/fiche brought about savings in utilization of space and were used initially for reports and newspapers collections. Thus, the application of any one of the newly emerging technologies, sing[illegible] and in isolation, to one or two areas of library and inform[illegible] studies, amounted to experimental work and posed to problems at all.

Computer Technology for Libraries

With rapid strides in technological revolution, computer hardware costs had declined at the rate of 30 to 40 per cent annually in the 1980s. computing costs had decreased by a factor of 10 every 4 years during the last three decades and the number of circuits per square millimeter on a computer chip doubless every year. Technology is now available to continue these trends forward for the next decade. While computational speed increased by a factor of 200 in 25 years, the cost of energy consumption and size of computers of comparable power came down by a factor of 10,000. The implication is that the storage of large volumes of full texts, which was once thought of as extremely prohibitive and practically not viable in the 1960s and 70s, has now become possible. All document transmission taking place physically is gradually being replaced by high-speed facsimile at a fraction of the cost and time. Telecommunications satellites, optical fibre cables providing tens of thousands of telecom channels, globally interconnected telecom system, digitization of all forms of information-voice, picture, text and computer data-and packet switching of these digitized information have transformed the nature of the telecom network. The telecom network has now become a transportation medium for information, which is more and more rapidly getting dematerialized from books, papers, and films.

The number of on-line databases derived from abstracting and indexing journals has been multiplying and on-line cataloguing data is being made available for the vast majority of documents acquired by libraries throughout the world through MARC-files or OCLC-like cooperative consortia/network. With the advancement of technology in providing digitized document delivery services of transmission at the national, regional or any geographic level, the focus in the coming decade will be on network of information and networking of people. The recent introduction of databases in compact discs (CD-ROM) will obviate the need to use telecommunication devices across the globe and may facilitate access to information at the local level, with only a personal computer on hand. Thus, the rapid evolution and convergence of many disparate technologies such as computers and telecommunications, augmented by micro computes, micro-eletronics, video and optical discs and advanced communication system—all applied in combination and in random – have brought about profound changes on every aspect of library.

The present IT revolution is inescapable and is certainly here to stay. It affects the availability of and access to information in which the library also has a role.

Libraries in 21st Century

The information industry in the West, of which libraries and information purveyors are only a small parts, dominates all other service sectors of the economy. In the emerging information conscious society, each country will set its own pace with its technological and manpower resources at command, attaching special importance to information as a catalyst in the socio-economic, scientific-technological, political and cultural processes of development of the society. In the developing economies, the information society will depends, to a great extent, on the library. A futuristic exotica of a 'paperless society' or bypassing of the library has been prognosticated and the technologically advanced academician, scientist or engineer may resort to such a 'State of the art' development, sitting at his terminal in his terminal in his home, office or laboratory. But for the majority of the use community, library will be one institution where information can be had, fee of cost or at nominal charges. The co-existence of literates, illiterates and neoliterates in India and other countries will necessitate the continuance of printed word and library resources for few more decades.

The libraries of tomorrow, however, will not be the same as we see them today. In line with the evolutionary nature of the communication media and the importance that has been assigned to them progressively by the user community, the priorities in the allocation of the scarce library budgetary resources have already shifted from printed books to periodicals and will soon drift to electronic databases services. Naturally, the collection of printed materials in each of the libraries will be minimal, retaining only those judged to be extremely relevant and most needed locally. Since this collection will meet only a small-portion of varied information requests or demands interdependence of libraries and sharing of resources will become very common. We have paid only lip service so far on these aspects through repeated academic discussions.

without being pragmatic. The resource sharing will be through network to union catalogues, union lists of printed books and periodicals held in other libraries or to directories of databases and their hosts, databases on research projects, institutions, experts and so forth. In such an environment, libraries will function as switching centers for information. Some of the libraries may even be involved in the development of indigenous databases for special, primary data collected and processed locally. Thus, a library will be a blend of the traditional collection along with an array of electronic storage and networking devices and terminals of serve as a switching center or interface for outside information.

House Keeping Work through Computers

With automation taking care of much of the house-keeping and routine library operations, librarianship will be freed from much of the clerical work and more attention could be paid to the intellectual aspects of information-related problems and services thereof. Due to the expected wider use of networks and the externally generated databases and cataloguing data, there will be a reduction in technical services. There will be a distinct move away from conventional librarianship and better management skills with background in IT handling and subject specialization will be expected of the professionals manning the library. The redeeming feature, even in the overshadowing of the conventional printed materials, is that the intellectual processing of the documents or queries input to the electronic systems, such as conceptual analysis, vocabulary control wherever required, thesaurus construction and maintenance, formulation of search strategies and user-system interface will have to be done by librarians and other information specialists. In the expanding information market place in the West, librarians constitute only less than 10 per cent of the workforce involved in information-related occupations and this proportion is expected to decrease over the years. Perhaps the situation is not so alarming in India but the librarians will have to compete with other information professionals drawn from diverse fields. Librarians, surveys have shown, can be more easily taught online techniques than teaching professional librarianship skills to an online technician or an individual subject enquirer. So librarianship skills are rated higher than subject knowledge in online searching.

Though a computer is versatile, it is not infallible and the computerized information sources are as reliable as the printed reference sources the librarians are familiar with. The new era of networking and computerised does not exist. Reference librarians develop through experience the ability to know the reliability of sources and comprehensiveness in coverage in answering particular type of enquiries.

The dichotomy between the teaching of library science and information science courses in the Universities will continue for several more years in the transition period. But a proper appreciation of both the manual and machine retrieval system will still be the basis on which the continued existence of librarians will rest. Constant updating of skills and retraining will be required. The subject specialists in the library profession will move into special, industrial or governmental libraries and the generalists drift into public or other libraries to provide community information services, services to economically underprivileged, materials for recreation and general study purposes. Whatever be the type of library, the future role of librarians as intermediaries or teachers and trainees of and users needs special mention.

3

Computer in Libraries: Indian Scenario

Introduction

We are experiencing the impact of the new technology on every facet of information handling. The advent of digital computer has opened up new possibilities in information management, and it is likely to change the information infrastructure by merging itself with other related technologies. The increasing use of computer systems for the control of management of information has important implications for our thinking about information. And this information processing, storage, and dissemination with the aid of computer is probably called the Information Technology.

Computers in India

The first computer in India, imported from the UK, was installed at the Indian Statistical Institute (ISI), Calcutta in 1955. And in the first decade since (1955-64) as many as 16 computers were installed in different parts of India.

The first indigenous computer was designed in India in 1964 by the ISI, Calcutta in collaboration with the Jadavpur University, Calcutta. This was the introductory phase for computer systems in

India, and since then India did not look back in the field of computerization. During the period 1965-72 the process of computerization speeded up with the installation of 170 more computer systems, although most of them were imported from the Western countries.

The Government of India gave the responsibility of the computers to the Department of Electronics which looked into the question of computer acquisition and evaluation. In 1975 the Government of India set up the National Informatics Centre at New Delhi, and two years later NICNET which now is proposed to be extended to each state capital and district level. Besides, many more computer networks have been established in India during the last decade or so. These include, in addition to the NICNET, the INDONET – it is the commercial network for the country as a whole. We have the RAILNET – it is the computer network for the railways; OILNET – computer network for oil sector; EDUNET – computer network for linking educational institutions; another related one is ERNET – computer network for education and research purposes; IANET – computer network for India Airlines, etc. Besides, there are others which are being developed as the BANKNET for the banking services; STEELNET for linking steel works across the country to form a communications network; etc.

Computers in Libraries

In India computers have already invaded the library and information field, and some of the libraries in the special and research organizations have introduced computer systems to automate some of their functions. These functions include book ordering and acquisition, cataloguing, serial control, circulation, generation and publication of bibliographies, indexes, and other documentation lists etc.

The following operations of the library functions cn be speedily processed by the computer. These are outlined briefly.

A. Acquisition

(i) Duplication checking
(ii) Preparation of order lists
(iii) Sending orders to book supplier/s

(iv) Monitoring orders and follow up action
(v) Verification with order file and invoices

B. Cataloguing

(i) Duplicating cataloguing cards
(ii) Preparation of authority file/subject heading list
(iii) Sorting, checking, and filing of catalogue cards
(iv) Automatic generation of added entries
(v) Generating the monthly accession lists

C. Circulation Control

(i) Registration of members
(ii) Charging and Discharging of documents
(iii) Updating the records file
(iv) Preparation of reminders
(v) Maintaining statistics
(vi) Information retrieval, etc.

D. Serial Control

(i) Ordering of serials
(ii) Receipt and updating the record file
(iii) Receipt to vendors/ publishers
(iv) List of holdings
(v) Preparing list of additions
(vi) Preparing list of binding

E. Documentation and Information Retrieval

(i) Indexing of micro and macro documents
(ii) Thesaurus construction
(iii) Abstracting work
(iv) Compilation of union catalogues/lists
(v) Bibliographic work

Advantages

The application of computer in libraries has enormous advantages. The various functions of a library can be extended further for the benefit of the users. Not that computerization will solve all the library problems with which it is infested today, but certainly it has great many potentialities as we have just seen above. If the librarian will be able to improve over the existing set of library services the image of the library and that of the librarian will definitely go up. Therefore some of the advantages of computerization are enumerated below:

(i) Increase in Speed and Saving of Time: Library computerization saves time in storing the information, information handling and information retrieval, etc. because all these functions are done at enormous speed. As a result, the time lag between the acquisition of documents and their availability to the users will be reduced considerably. And, computer networking will further help in saving time of the library personnel and the users.

(ii) Computer system: will lend in updating the record files much more quickly and easily than in the manual system.

(iii) Greater Library Cooperation: With the installation of computer system in libraries in the country as a whole, the opportunities of library cooperation will increase. These computer systems installed in differet institutions can be hooked to each other via satellite and through a central agency, and thereby can know each other's collection. Library cooperation can be achieved at various levels and for different functions including acquisitions, cataloguing, linter-library lending etc.

(iv) Better Library Management: When properly planned, per unit operating costs will normally be reduced by computerization. The money thus saved can be utilize for some other productive purposes, such as book purchase, or starting a new service for users, etc.

(v) Staffing: In order to meet with the increasing needs for services, the use of equipment can further be extended as such scope always exists in the system. There is, therefore, no need for increasing the manpower.

(vi) New Services: Many new services can be introduced without any extra cost or manpower. And many library services can be generated only as a by product of the records already available on the system.

(vii) Report Production: Various types of reports about library activities, and other letters, follow up notices, sending of reminders, etc can automatically be generated.

Indian Scenario

(i) INSDOC, New Delhi: This national level documentation center has been compiling a National Union Catalogue of Scientific Serials in India with the help of a computer. Another application of the computer has been the compilation of the Author Index and the key-word based Subject index of the Indian Science Abstracts. Thus computerization helps in the easy retrieval of information. INSDOC has also pioneered the computerized SDI service in 1975 when it started with CAN/SDI software.

(ii) National Aeronautical Lab., Bangalore: In the library of this organization use of computer system has been made for circulation control, document ordering, acquisition of library material, and information retrieval.

(iii) BARC, Bombay: At this research center of atomic energy of atomic energy, computer has been put to use for cataloguing its technical reports. It is now serving as the inputting center to INIS at the international level.

(iv) DRTC, Bangalore: Computer is being used at the DRTC for document finding, and also for the training of its trainees.

The also use computer for the purpose of giving short term courses to working librarians.

They are also storing data about Colon Classification on computer for the production of schedules. It can also help in automatic classification.

(v) SERC, Roorkee: For the retrieval of bibliographic information a computer system is made available at the library of the Structural Engineering Research Center, Roorkee.

(vi) CFTRI, Mysore: A National Information Center for food Science & Technology has been developed at the CFTRI. Its library provides computerized Current Awareness Services to the CFTRI and its work stations, food industry and other R&D organizations. It also provides on-line search facilities on the database developed. At present it is serving as inputting centre to International Food Information Service (IFIS) for India.

(vii) Central Drug Research Institute, Lucknow: The National Information Centre here has developed a non-bibliographical database on medicinal plants. It has successfully developed and

implemented softwares for library automation, natural products and patents search through online access.

(viii) Central Leather Research Institute, Madras: For its library it has planned computerized SDI service. It has developed a database for a variety of uses, particularly for information retrieval. It has been generating the annual cumulative subject indices for the service, Current Leather Literature.

(ix) Central Machine Tools Institute, Bangalore: It has been using computer system for data storage, retrieval, online processing of technical enquiries and library transactions.

(x) ATIRA, Ahmedabad: A Selective Dissemination of Information services is in operation using a computer system available at ATIRA, the national information centre for textiles.

(xi) IIS, Bangalore: In its library, the automate circulation system has been developed and implemented.

(xii) IIT, New Delhi: It has developed and implemented a computerized circulation control system as a part of the computerization.

(xiii) SAIL, Ranchi: For its library and information centre, it has developed a computerized document acquisition system database.

(xiv) DESIDOC, Delhi: For its library it has developed and implemented a computerized document acquisition system database, among others.

(xv) BHEL, Bangalore: Here also a computerized book acquisition system has been developed and implemented.

In addition to the above, there are scores of more special libraries and information centers attached to the research organizations which have either developed computerized system or at the planning stage and would develop soon according to their requirements.

(i) Anna University library, Madras: The circulation service and the information retrieval functions have been computerized in this University Library successfully.

(ii) Punjab University Library, Chandigarh: It has also installed a microcomputer and has input the periodicals records in the system for efficiency and better control. It is planning to extend its applications in the library.

(iii) Gandhi Vidyapeeth, Ahmedabad: When this author visited its Library in March 1988, it had already acquired a computer system and was at the planning stage.

(iv) Punjabi University Library, Patiala: It has also acquired a computer system in order to computerize some of its operations. It is in the process of giving training to some of its staff.

(v) JNU Library, New Delhi: This University Library has also acquired a computer system for automating its library functions.

These are just some examples. There are other university libraries which are in the process of acquiring one or the other computer system for computerizing the housekeeping jobs. In this region, as per the knowledge of the author, some more university libraries are planning to go for computerization, and for this purpose they are trying to give hands-on training to their staff. Moreover, the UGC has already approved the development of information and library network for the Eighth Five Year Plan period, which will give incentive to other university libraries in the country to buy the computers. It is, therefore, hoped that during the Eighth Five Year Plan all the 170 university libraries will acquire computer system as envisaged under the ambitious INFLIBNET network system whereby all of them will be linked to each other in order to share resources and make the whole country a very vast library. This network will also be extended to include about 500 colleges, and about 200 R&D centers to make it more worthwhile and viable network.

4

Computer Software for Indian Libraries

Overview

The sectoral documentation centres reflect the 'discipline-oriented' (education, social science, communication, etc.) nature of Unesco. As a result, the decentralised documentation network: (i) allows the organisation to channel the documentation flow along the lines of a given discipline and tb make a local decision on what to put into the system; (ii) ensures the speedy processing of new materials and the updating of the data bases; and (iii) promotes a close relationship with the users and effectively serves them with relevant information. The responsibility for the functioning and the co-ordination of the network is entrusted to the Division of Library, Archives and Documentation Services (LAD). LAD also provides methodological and technical assistance, offers training courses, seminars and furthers the development of the CDS/ISIS software underlying the network.

Acquisitions

The fundamental process in establishing and maintaining a documentation network consists of a uniform acquisition policy. In Unesco, such a policy:

(i) ensures that the overall collection meets the information needs of Unesco;

(ii) is geard to the programme and objectives of the organisation; and

(iii) eliminates little used and/or obsolete material.

Acquisition materials in Unesco are derived from two sources: internal material generated by the organisation (e.g. Unesco publications and documents), and external material (e.g. reference material: general dictionaries, encyclopedias, directories, ete., and subject-oriented, such as textbooks, handbooks, manuals, standards on a specialised subject), as well as relevant monographs, periodicals and documents published commercially, or produced by national and international organisations and bodies.

Selection of Books

Once material has been selected, ordered and received, it must be processed. Over the years, Unesco has developed comprehensive facilities for the processing of the acquired material. Cataloguing rules, adhering to international standard practices, have been designed explicitly for machine-readable cataloguing and have been adapted to the computerised bibliographic data bases developed within Unesco. Although a given classification scheme may be used for subject retrieval, most existing computerised documentation systems use keyword subject indexing for retrieval. Within the context of the Unesco documentation network classification schemes are used only for shelving purposes.

Depending on the type of material, the following classification schemes are used: (i) monographs, Universal Decimal Classification (UDC); (ii) Unesco documents (hard copy), document number; (iii) Unesco documents (microfiches), microfiche number; (iv) documents issued by international organisations other than Unesco: for hard copy, issuing body (e.g. United Nations) and document code; for microfiches, issuing body and microfiche number.

Most current bibliographic information systems in existence are based on the use of a thesaurus (a structured list of controlled terms) for assigning descriptors/keywords to an item in order to identify its subject content and to ensure its retrieval. The Unesco Thesaurus is a structured list of descriptors for indexing and retrieving literature in the fields of education, science and social science, culture and communication. It is considered the basic terminological reference work to be used within the Unesco documentation network, either alone or in conjunction with other thesauri designed to cover specific subject fields. Each sectoral documentation centre is responsible for processing (cataloguing, classifying, indexing and data base entry) the material in its field of competence.

Computerize Services

The final objective of any documentation network is to satisfy the demands for information placed upon it. Each Unesco sectoral documentation centre may provide:

1. Search formulation and inquiry services that answer requests and/or provide relevant Unesco publications and documents.
2. Bibliographic services, including (i) manual/computerised literature searches, (ii) computer-produced bibliographies (retrospective search services), and (iii) selective dissemination of information (SDI) services.
3. Dissemination of information, including distribution of accession lists prepared by the documentation centres and/or provision of lists of secondary literature.
4. Adjust services, including (i) editing (microthesauri, directories, newsletters, etc.), and (ii) provision of mailing lists, lists of meetings, experts, etc.

In developing the aforementioned services the present and future sectoral documentation centres of Unesco will increasingly rely on: (i) printed catalogues (in microfiche form) of the holdings of the centre; (ii) online terminals for direct access to the various Unesco data bases; and (iii) bibliographies on specific subjects, current awareness lists, etc., produced by the centres themselves.

THE UNESCO CDS/ISIS

History

The Computerised Documentation System (CDS) was established in 1971 to provide the Member States with information on Unesco's programme as reflected in its publications and documents, to permit the Unesco Secretariat members and consultants to have access to different types of information stored in Unesco's data bases, and to function as a demonstration and training centre for the application of advanced computerisation techniques in information processing, storage and retrieval.

The CDS data bases consist of the following Unesco materials: (i) General Conference documents; (ii) Executive Board documents; (iii) Secretariat documents (including working and main series documents, field-mission reports, reports of meetings and conferences, sectoral, divisional and international documents); (iv) documents of regional offices and/or affiliated institutes, and (v) publications (monographs and periodicals). The data bases also include the acquisitions of the Unesco Library and a selection of documents and publications emanating from international organisations. At the request of Unesco Member States (e.g. National Commissions for Unesco, Permanent Delegations to Unesco and Unesco depository libraries), as well as national government bodies, universities and research institutions, the Unesco Secretariat and organisations of the United Nations system, the data bases can be searched and SDI services provided.

Growth & Development of CDS/ISIS

The original CDS version was developed to run on the ICL 1903A computer. In 1975, Unesco decided to replace its ICL computer with an IBM computer. The two computers being incompatible, CDS faced the problem of converting the ICL computers package it had developed to IBM package. At that point, CDS decided to adopt an early version of this ISIS (Integrated Set of Information Systems) developed by the International Labour Organisation (ILO). But since ISIS lacked many of the features which the ICL programmes-had, a major re-design was required.

Development work on ISIS began at Unesco early in 1975. Unesco invested about eight man-years and changed about 80 percent of the original ISIS software received from ILO before the present CDS/ISIS system became operational at the end of 1975. A completely new, online subsystem using CICS (Customer Information Control System) with sophisticated data entry and retrieval facilities was developed for CDS/ISIS; and printing facilities, including photocomposition, were extended. The concept of modularity has been adopted to minimize the cost of changes that from time to time need to be introduced. One of the principal advantages of CDS/ISIS is that the same set of computer programmes is used to manipulate various data bases, each of which may be composed of a quite different data content, This means that expensive reprogramming is not needed whenever a new data base for a new project must be established.

Data exchange between cooperating institutions is one of the most important problems in the field of information storage and retrieval. Frequently, data bases produced by other institutions could be used to expand and enhance an existing data base. But to take advantage of data externally produced, the receiving institution must convert the incoming data into its own processing format. To facilitate the exchange of information between different systems, the International Organization for Standardization (ISO) has developed a standard format for data interchange. (ISO/2709-1973, Documentation-Format for Bibliographic Information Interchange on Magnetic Tape.) Originally designed for bibliographic data, it now appears that a much more general use can be made of this standard format to transmit virtually any kind of data.

About the CDS/ISIS

CDS/ISIS is a computer-based system for information storage, processing and retrieval. 1t is a generalised system that can handle any alphanumeric data of fixed or variable lengths. It has a comprehensive collection of programmes for input, management and output; these programmes run in batch or online modes. The key to the systems is the file structure, which consists of a number of computer files logically related but physically distinct. The structure permits the users to add, modify and delete whole or parts of records in a batch or an online mode; to keep the data base current through updating of the master file and other files, and to search and retrieve information in either mode through the use of search terms and Boolean expressions. The file structure also allows users to gain access to the master file via any element in the corresponding data base; to build indexes from keywords, thesaurus terms, or from a free text; to specify sorting and printing instructions, and to create a variety of print formats for specialised types of output such as reports, catalogues, indexes.

CDS/ISIS is an integrated system and data entered can be used in any number of processes. During online operation, users are guided and prompted at their terminal by the system. The system runs on IBM 360, 370 or 303X computers and on RIAD 1035, 1040, 1060 computers operating under the Operating System (OS/MFT, MVT, VS1, or V5).

For data storage, the system supports IBM 2314, 3330, 33340 or other compatible direct access device. At least one disc drive and two magnetic tape drives are required.

The online processors support IBM 3270s or compatible terminals such as the Memorex 1377, teletypes and teletype-compatible terminals, and IBM 2741s. The online processors are written in Assembler languager and operate under CICS (Customer Information Control System), an IBM proprietory data base/data communication system. CICS is used for task, terminal and data management services. The access methods used are: SAM, DAM, PAM and ISAM.

The batch programme requires a partition (or region) of approximately I50 K although many programmes will run in a smaller region.

The storage required by the online processors may vary widely, depending on the user requirements, and the number of terminals and/or data bases operated simultaneously. A dynamic area of at least 50 K should be made available within the CICS partition (over and above CICS's own requirements).

CDS/ISIS has a facility for recording diacritical marks and displaying diacritical mark codes (normally for the purpose of proof-reading the data), displaying the actual accented character (provided a suitable print train is available) or suppressing them.

Furthermore when data bases containing confidential information are created and/or searched online, CCS/ISIS provides facilities to protect the privacy of such data bases. Protection is ensured by means of 'passwords' which the terminal operator must supply in order to be able to have access to a given data base. A data base may be protected in terms of updating and for retrieval, or both. Updating protection enables the ISIS user to authorise only certain persons to create and/or modify records of a data base.

CDS/ISIS Operations

As CDS/ISIS developed and became operational, various units of the Unesco Secretariat seeking to establish specialised information systems increasingly began to use the system.

CDS	Unesco Bibliographic Data Base, Unesco Publications and Documents, Unesco Library Acquisitions.
CDTHES	Unesco Thesaurus.
DARE	Experts, institutions, research projects, documents and journals in the field of the social sciences.
ISORID	Research projects and reports in the field of libraries, documentation and archives.
EDFAC	Basic references on educational facilities.
IEEN	Experts and institutions in the field of environmental education.
UNEP	Industry and environment (operated by the Paris Office of UNEP).

In addition to the Secretariat of Unesco, Unesco Member States and various organisations in the United Nations family increasingly request the CDS/ISIS software. In response to this interest Unesco has established a procedure for transferring the CDS/ISIS software free of charge to organisations in Unesco Member States and in the United Nations family.

Following the agreement to transfer the CDS/ISIS software, and prior to the actual installation, project personnel of the receiving institution are instructed in the operation of the system. Normally, such instruction takes . the form of a three-week training course to enable the participants to install and use the package in a relatively short time. For a number of years Unesco has offered such courses in the spring (April-May) and autumn (October-November), usually in Paris. Depending on the background of the participants, the emphasis of the course is on guided, practical work, touching upon all the major system components.

The system is usually installed by the trained project personnel. Once an expert from Unesco evaluates the initial operation of the system, the new installation is considered to be autonomous, i.e., not requiring further direct assistance.

Unesco does, however, ensure close contact with CDS/ISIS users concerning the maintenance and updating of the system carried out within Unesco. Users are regularly kept informed of system developments by circular letters. Unesco maintains a special CDS/ISIS System Maintenance Data Base (SMDB), which records all system changes. The print-outs and indexes of SMDB are regularly sent to all users.

Every installation is also followed up through (a) visits of Unesco experts at the various installations; (b) technical advice by mail, telex or telephone; and (c) regular shipment of new system releases and related, up-to-date documentation to every installation.

In addition to the manuals described above, Unesco also issues Technical Notes to cover specific technical topics, guidelines and procedures concerning the system. All manuals are maintained in machine-readable form (for the time being, in English only) and are regularly updated as new features and/or system changes are implemented. The manuals are stored on the system tape together with the CDS/ISIS programme and catalogue procedures.

Development of CDS/ISIS

In order to develop the CDS/ISIS to the level of sophistication required, the following plans are envisaged:

1. Develop a fully automatic multilingual Unesco Thesaurus handling capability (including thesaurus maintenance, thesaurus-aided indexing and retrieval).
2. Extend data-base capability to an unlimited number of records and unlimited size of the records (for the time being, the maximum number of records per data base is 100,000; the number of data bases is unlimited).
3. Extend the capabilities of the system to process not only bibliographic but also substantive information elements.
4. Ensure a compatibility between CDS/ISIS and the MINISIS (minicomputer-based information system), developed by the International Development Research Centre (IDRS) and run on a Hewlett Packard 3000 (Series II and III minicomputers).
5. Study the feasibility of converting CDS/ISIS for use on other minicomputers.

5

Implementation of Computer Software in Libraries

Definition

Software refers to computer programmes, procedures, rules and associated documentation and data pertaining to the operation of a computer system. In contrast to hardware components of a computer which can be seen and felt, software is not directly tangible. But without software computers can not do any useful work. A good analogy is the Lighting system in a house. Switches, bulbs and connecting wires are the hardware components. But they need electricity to work, of which we are not always aware.

Types of Software

Software can be categorised into two types: (a) System software which consists of programmes needed for functioning of the computer and to provide user-computer interfaces. Such software is generally supplied and maintained by the manufacturers. Choice of hardware usually determines the type of system software-operating system, programmes, compilers I/O routines, memory and file management, utilities like word processing, spread sheets, data base management, editor, sorting, etc.; (b) Application software: Computer programmes developed to perform tasks specific to the individual user or an institution, etc.

Acquisition through Computer

1. Turn-key system approach where a system is designed, marketed and maintained by a vendor who supplies a complete system of software and hardware to perform a defined application.
2. Custom designed for a particular computer system or a range of computer systems by a software vendor either by developing a completely new package or by tuning an existing package.
3. Bought off-the-shelf from a software vendor along with necessary documentation for installation, usage and maintenance.

Computer Software for Library

Library Management (House-keeping functions)

- Cataloguing
- Circulation
- Acquisition
- Serials control

Management Support

- Statistics
- MIS
- Accounting
- Budget control

Data Base Management Support and Information Retrieval (DBMS&IR)

- Data base creation
- Searching

Generation of information products like CAS, SDI, indexes and Bibliographies

- Thesaurus maintenance
- Directory generation, etc.

Purpose of Software

Several software directories, both general and specific to L&I work are available for identification, selection and procurement of software packages. Special mention must be made here of the UNISIST 'international Inventory of Software Packages in Information Field', which gives details of 188 softwrare packages for L&I work. Such directories are also made available as data base fifes for online searching by vendors like DIALOG, BRS, etc.

Under general purpose software, one can mention word processors (e.g. WORDSTAR), data base management systems (e.g. DBASE II & TII), spread sheets (e.g. SUPERCALC) and graphics packages. These can be used as tools for developing a broad range of applications.

Software can also be developed taking into consideration the needs of a particular application or user group, e.g., a serials management system for a library. The need for developing such an application dependent package becomes essential when general purpose software tools fail to meet the desired requirements of the application. The nature of data involved in L&I work and the type of operations performed on this data necessitate the need for developing software specific to these requirements. This is not, however, to mean that there is no role for software like word processors and DBMS in L&I work. They can definitely be used profitably whenever a situation demanding their need arises.

Growth & Development of Software

Software development is largely targeted to users in business, government, educational and R&D establishments. Majority of the applications are Management Information System (MTS) or scientific and engineering in nature. Although this is true largely in developed countries also, there are several software houses and vendors specialising in L&I software development in USA and UK. It will take some more time before the software industry in India can enter into this sector due to lack of sufficient user demands. Factors like wide spread availability of cheap computer hardware, increasing awareness of their usage in libraries should definitely hasten this process. Considering the number of libraries, there is a vast scope for L&T software market in the country.

At present the Indian library professionals have taken recourse to two alternatives for obtaining software for L&T work: (i) developed internally by the library staff or EDP staff' in the parent organisation, and (ii) obtained freely or at nominal cost from professional societies, other organisations, individuals or from international agencies like UNESCO; etc. There are very few instances where a library has purchased a commercially available package.

In the private sector, the author knows of only one company, Informatics India (Pvt) Ltd., Bangalore, which acts as a software vendor for two software packages SCIMATE (produced by LS.T., USA) and 1NMAGTC (produced by INMAGIC Inc., USA). SCIMATE has been purchased by a few libraries and information centres.

Financial Problem with Software

The cost of software has tended to rise at least 10 per cent annually while the cost of the hardware is decreasing at a much faster rate of 30-40%. Dramatic advancements have been made in computer hardware technology (processing and storage capabilities) due to the research work carried out in micro-electronics. Improvements of the same magnitude have not taken place on the software side although much research work is being done on software development techniques which have an effect on the programmer productivity.

Software development still involves the classical steps of analysis, requirements specification, system design, software development, testing and .refining, installation and maintenance. These steps are essentially labour intensive involving the efforts of several experts. It has been the common exprience that most of the software development projects tend to overstep the estimated cost and time frames.

Software costs related to L&I field can serve as an illustration. The UNISIST directory gives the following cost break-up for those L&I software packages that reported prices:

Free (Source or object)	-	17
Under $ 5000	-	20
$ 5001-10,000	-	14
$ 10,001-50,000	-	28
$ 50,001-100,000	-	11
Over $ 100,000	-	3
Lease only (source or object)	-	S

Design of Software

Another major problem area is that there are few software packages that are truly portable. This means that one has to take into consideration the cost of the hardware if the same is not already available to the library. An example in case is the MINISIS package, made available free of cost to the non-profit institutions in developing countries by IDRC, Canada. Although it is quite a sophisticated package which has proven its worth at several installations around the world, it requires a HP 3000 minicomputer system which means an expenditure of several lakhs of rupees in installation, training, maintenance, etc.

Software Duplicating of Software

Software piracy is a phenomenon prevalent in all countries, more so in developing countries due to the absence of strict controls in illegal copying, duplication and usage of popular packages. Particularly with the easy availability of IBM/PC compatible microcomputers in India, the market is being flooded with a wide variety of software, tempting a person to obtain a free copy of a package from his friend or an unscrupulous vendor. But this can lead to unhappy situations in the long run. Besides the potential legal problems involved, there will be problems regarding maintenance and servicing in cases of any breakdowns.

Hardware Problems

Till now, non-availability of suitable computer hardware at reasonable prices had been the main bottle-neck for Indian libraries intending to go in for automation. With the recent liberalisation of GOI policies related to import, manufacture, etc. of computers/ components, there has been a fantastic growth in the industry towards making available reasonably priced computers in the market.

The higher end micros (of IBM-PC/AT type) available in the Indian market are capable of meeting both the functional and financial requirements of majority of the libraries. It is also understood that licence has been issued for indigenous manufacture of Micro-VAX-II, a 32 bit micro by DEC which is completely code compatible with VAX-11/780 systems. Several Indian companies are also offering 32 bit micro systems based on standard processors like Motorola 68020, Intel 80386, with standard operating systems like UNIX.

Contribution of PGI/UNESCO

A major source of encouragement for libraries in developing countries is the efforts made my PGI/UNESCO within the UNISIST framework to make available software packages and the associated documentation, training, etc., free of cost. Three software packages of particular interest are:

1. CDS/ISIS (Main frame, mini and micro versions)
2. SUPERDOC (Microcomputers)
3. IV + V (Microcomputers-under testing)

Brief features of CDS/ISIS and 5UPERDOC are shown in Annexure on next page. All the three software packages are currently available in India through the UNISIST national focal point at Department of Scientific and Industrial Research, Government of India. Although the current-versions -of these packages are intended mainly for data base creation and information retrieval, UNESCO has plans to augment CDS/ISIS micro version with software routines for house-keeping operations like serials control, acquisition, etc.

How to Tackle Software Problems?

Following are a few concrete steps which are suggested for improving the situation related to L&I software in India. Plans for implementing such steps should ideally be evolved as collaborative efforts between agencies like NI5SAT (DSIR), ILA, IASLIC, and research and educational institutions.

1. Introduce papers on computer programming, library automation, software packages, etc., at B.Lib.Sc and M.Lib.Sc levels with particular attention to practical orientation. Library schools should have their own hardware for this purpose.
2. Collaborate closely with agencies like UNESCO in popularising software packages like CDS/ISIS and SUPERDOC in India.
3. Develop software for house-keeping routines in a high level language for IBM/PC compatible micros and make these available for interested institutions.

4. Develop a core group of specialists in computer application to L&I field who can be called upon to provide consultancy, training, installation, etc.
5. Discourage librarians from using illegally acquired software for developing and installing production systems.
6. Organise training courses for working librarians with greater emphasis on practicals on using software packages.
7. Provide intensive courses on computer software and hardware to selected L&I science teachers who are identified to teach these to the students.
8. Bring out printed guides to automation in libraries on topics such as use of word processing, DBMS and spread sheets criteria for selecting hardware and software use of software packages like CDS/ISIS programming for L&I work, etc.

6

Information Technology for Libraries

Overview

In the past the volume of information was not as large as it is today, and the libraries were in a position to organize the information materials through manual operation. But since the Second World War there has been a tremendous output of information, which has been usually referred to as information explosion. The materials of information in both print and non-print media – manuscripts, books, journals, reports, films, discs, tapes (i.e. a variety of information packages) – continue to be produced and used in greater and greater quantities. As Xerox Corporation put it in one of their promotional brochures in 1984, 'Recorded Knowledge has doubled during the last twelve years. It will double again during the next ten'. Charles L. Bernier informs us that about 2,000,000 biomedical papers were published annually in 1964 in 70 languages and about 500,000 chemical papers were published in 1976. This vast amount of information has to be processed, stored and retrieved whenever required. The very complexity and magnitude of the problem makes it an impossible task to process by manual method. Library and information scientists are increasingly being compelled to take the help of semiautomatic and automatic machines for information handling.

The revolutionary developments in information technology have two impacts. Firstly, as more and more information is readily available in machine-readable form, there has been a fundamental shift in the concerns of the information profession from 'more information' to 'accurate, up-to-date and timely information'. Secondly, as computers are used increasingly for provision of information, librarians and other information professionals must familiarize themselves with the latest technological development in this field.

Past of Computer Technology

Although credit goes to Charles Babbage; Professor of Mathematics at Cambridge University, who invented the first general purpose digital computer in 1822, it was during the Second World War that the first electronic computer, the ENIAC (Electronic Numerical Integrator and Calculator) was developed under the direction of J. W. Mauchly and J. P. Eckert, Jr. In 1945 the EDVAC (Electronic Discrete Variable Automatic Computer) was built embodying the ideas of John Von Neumann, the propounder of self-reproducing automata theory. Finally, in 1951, the first commercially available computer, the UNIVAC (Universal Automatic Computer) was installed in the U.S. Bureau of the Census.

The computers used during the period from 1951 to 1959 were known as the first generation of computers. The period from 1959 to 1964 could be considered to be the time of the second generation of computers, while 1964 could be considered as the birth year of the third and fourth generation of computers. For the first generation of computers vacuum tubes were used, while for the second generation, transistors and for the third and fourth generation, integrated or semi-conductor circuits are used.

The earlier systems were operated in an off-line batch processing mode. The technique required bringing of data to a data centre where it was punched on to cards and these were then read into the computer. The desired programme, usually stored in magnetic tape, was also selected and entered from the tape into the computer memory. The programme acted on the data and the results of the processing were output via a printer. The system developed by the National Library of Medicine (USA) —Medical Literature Analysis and Retrieval System (MEDLARS) – was the largest computerized retrieval system through off-line batch processing method.

The term 'on line' refers to the searcher being in direct communication with the system he wishes to use.. It facilitates searching without a formal batch operation. The user provides input to the system and it, in turn, reports back to the user. In such a system the processing time of the computer can be shared by several users simultaneously. The first large-scale on line information storage and retrieval system was the Remote Console (RECON) system of NASA. This system became fully operational in 1969. Since then hundreds of databases in different fields have become available for on line searching of bibliographic information. The most important example is provided by OCLC project of the USA. Based at Ohio, the project became operational in 1971, with the objective of creating a centralized on line cataloguing system.

The late 1960s also saw the introduction of mini-computers. These were initially developed as low-cost computers with a minimum of processing power and memory. Rapid developments in microelectronics technology in late seventies resulted in micro-computers, personal computers and so on. Mini-computers, micro-computers and microprocessors are mostly used for dedicated type of work either as stand alone computers or linked to a big computer. A micro-processor is a low-cost machine which requires programmes to be written in a machine language. A micro-computer is a small and inexpensive computer. The capabilities of micro- computers are increasing so fast that the distinction between mini-computer and micro-computer has narrowed down considerably. The potential of the micro-computer has expanded in recent years with the ability to interface with other computers and systems and by the linking of machines to provide distributed processing. It is anticipated that by the end of the century the capabilities of microcomputers will approximate to those of present day large computers. The development has the effect of minimizing the computer cost.

Word Processors are special purpose micro-computers dedicated to a single function: the processing of text. It drastically reduces the time in producing neat and error-free reports. The material once typed into the system can be modified, altered or edited without retyping the whole material. A word processor can also be linked to a full-time computer. Word processing systems can play important roles in information handling.

Computer output to microfilm/microfiche (COM) is a device which converts a computer output to a photographic image on microfilm/microfiche.

TYPES OF COMPUTER TECHNOLOGY

Laser Computer Technology

Laser scan or laser-read medium are now being used for storage of information. Optical digital discs (for text and print materials) and analog discs (for images) are currently being used in advanced countries for this purpose. The Library of Congress is reported to have introduced different types of digital optical and analog optical discs such as (a) acct Read After Write (DRAW); (b) Compact Disc Read Only memory (CD ROM); (c) Laser Videodisc: and (d) Audio Compact Disc (ACD). DRAW is a 12-inch laser-written and laser-read digital disc which can contain upto a gigabyte or 1 billion characters of digital data, which is equivalent to more than three copies o[the text of the 30-volume Encyclopedia Britannica in character form, or alternatively 10,000 digitized page of images. CD-ROM disc is generally smaller, 4.72 inch, which contains 5[illegible]0 megabytes of digital data equivalent to the complete text of two 30-volume sets of the Encyclopedia Britannica, or alternatively 5400 digitized page of images. CD-ROM can be read but not written upon by the user. The smaller size makes it more convenient for use with personal computers. As a replicable disc, CD-ROM is becoming the most important form of optical storage for distribution of database. A Laser Videodisc is an analog optical disc. It is a 12- inch replicable video disc which can contain either 30 minutes of motion picture material with two independent sound tracks or 54,000 separate colour still-frame images with no sound. An Audio Compact Disk is a smaller disc of 4.72 inch which contains digitized high fidelity music of mare than one hour's duration.

Micrographic Computer Technology

Micrography means miniaturization of documents. In micrographics documents are highly reduced in size and recorded on microfilm. A high precision camera and a special film are used to record the documents at high reduction. This precision camera is called microfilm camera and the special film is known as microfilm.

Microfilms are available in roll and sheer forms. Basically, there are two types of microfilm cameras: planetary type and rotary type. The former is used for microfilming larger documents and the latter, for smaller documents. Microfilms are normally available in roll and sheet forms. Roll microfilm consists of 16- mm and 35-mm film wound on an open spool. The former is used for recording small documents like books, journals, loose sheets, and so on, and the latter is used for recording large-size documents like newspapers, maps, or engineering drawings. Since documents arc recorded in sequential order in a roll of microfilm, one has to scan the roll from one end to the other to search a document. To overcome this difficulty roll films can be cut into strips and put into transparent holders or pockets. This is known as unitized microfilm, and a unitized holder may have 50 to 100 frames. A larger version of the strip is called aperture card. It normally consists of a single frame of 35-mm microfilm inserted in an acetate jacket. Aperture cards are normally used for the management of engineering drawings. But the most popular form of microfilm for library use is sheet microfilm or microfiche. A microfiche of the 'size of 4 by 6 inches can accommodate about 60 to $200 images (pages), depending upon the reduction ratio used at the time of filming. Microfiche can not only contain a large number of documents in a small area but also provide easy access to recorded information. It is not necessary here to discuss how microfilms are processed in a processor and stored in a cabinet But the important units of the micrographic system are' the microfilm reader, the microfilm reads printer, and the microfilm duplicator. Both reading the microfilm and getting a print-out on paper. A microfilm duplicator, on the other hand, is used for making duplicate copies of an existing microfilm for the purpose of replacement or for distribution.

Reprographic Computer Technology

Reprography means the reproduction of graphic materials which may be handwritten, typed or printed, Several processes and techniques have been developed to reproduce a faithful replica of an original document. The better known processes are (a) electrostatic process; (b) diazographic process; (c) thermographic process; and (d) silver halide process. Photocopying of documents is known as xerography. There are five operational steps involved in making xerox copies: charging, exposing, developing, transferring and fixing (on paper). There is a wide range of xerox machines that facilitate high/low volume copies with reduction/enlargement facilities. The quality of photo-conductive materials determines the quality of xerox copies. Normally plain bond-weight and dust-free paper is used for making xerox copies. Because the photo-conductive plates/drums, toner ink and paper are sensitive to heat, humidity and dust, they are operated in air-conditioned rooms.

The important duplication techniques are offset duplication, stencil duplication and spirit duplication. Offset duplication is a modified version of offset printing. It is a process in which the text of a document is transferred to a master/matrix consisting of a stiff shut of paper or thin aluminium. Thereafter, it is run on a machine to reproduce multiple copies. Stencil duplication is also known by the terms mimeograph and cyclostyling. Stencil for copying is prepared by hand, with the help of a typewriter and by using an electronic stencil-cutting machine. Then the prepared stencil is run on a machine to produce duplicate copies. The spirit duplication is also known as Hectography. It consists of a special carbon paper and receiver sheet. In place of normal carbon an alcohol (spirit) soluble dye is used, and the receiver sheet consists of a stiff glazed sheet of paper. This is the only process whereby different portions of a document can be duplicated in different colours by using different colour carbons while typing the desired portions of the master.

Telecommunication Computer Technology

The popularity of telephones in communication of information is well-known. It has been widely used for short and specific information in libraries. Postal services are used for dispatching books and other documents including photocopies of papers demanded by the outstation users. The introduction of the speed-post system has facilitated Quick transmission of information materials. This traditional mode of communication has been and will continue to be useful for sending large and bulky items. But the latest advance in communication technology is the introduction of the Fax machine. Fax machines transmit more directly between two parties, and are thus growing in popularity as a mode of communication for rendering library services.

Fax is a simple technology which sends facsimites, copies of paper or electronic documents, through telephone wires. It is a combination of modem and copier and, in some cases, micro-computer. There is a transmitting fax and a receiving fax and a transceiver fax which both transmits and receives. It is sometimes called telecopier. The first step in faxing a document is to scan it with the help of a scanner, usually built into a fax machine. A scanner's role is to convert paper documents into electronic documents. When a fax machine scans a document, it creates a digital copy consisting of hundreds of dots. Scanning is not necessary in a micro-computer fax operation because the electronic document is prepared by itself. The fax machine then converts this digital information into analog signals for transmission through telephone lines. The receiving fax converts the message back to digital form and prints it on paper. Fax messages are transmitted either by telephone networks or by digital data networks (DDN). The DDN are high-speed computer lines, not yet widely available. Transmission can be made in a minute or so under the former system and in a few seconds under the latter system. Not all fax machines are equal in resolution. Standard ones are 100 by 200 lines per inch (LPI) having differences in shades. Some fax machines use thermal paper and some, plain paper. It is easier to operate a stand-alone fax machine. Equipped with a fax modem, special fax circuit card, software and other hardware devices, a personal computer can offer greater flexibility with fax transmission.

Electronic mail (E-mail) is a form of computer transmission of messages. In E-mail messages can be sent via telephone lines in the form of computer data from one institution to another for quick communication. Teletext and Videotex are recent entrants to the information scene. Videotex or viewdata is an information system accessed via telephone network using a keypad and displayed on an adapted television receiver. A teletext is a non- interactive system linking the information provider to the home via a regular or cable TV broadcast signal. In both the cases TV sets with special decoders can pick up the message. Whereas Videotex is telephone-based, teletext is broadcast. The latter is more easily accessible and less expansive than the former. Both systems have significantly extended the range of information available to the public from their own homes.

Applications of Computer Technology for Library

A mainframe computer is used to create a large database. It manipulates bibliographical records in a machine-readable form. It can be updated at regular intervals. Once this is done a database is ready for exploitation. The databases can be used in a number of way. Firstly, they may be used for retrospective search of a specific topic. Secondly, a database can also be used for selective dissemination of information (SDI). In SDI, the current interests of users are defined in an 'interest profile' which is stored in a machine-readable form. After the database has been updated, the additions are checked against the interest profiles. Matching records are printed out and sent W the appropriate users. Thirdly, a database can be exploited through on line searching for quick and accurate information. The availability of on-line databases and services has given rise .to the establishment of library networks. The networks have made it possible for the participating libraries to share their resources with other libraries by avoiding duplication in acquisitions and to handle inter-Library loans and cooperative cataloguing in an on-line environment.

The large computers were originally applied for the traditional information handling works. But with the advent of mini-computers the scope of computerization has considerably widened. There are three basic types of a mini-computer system: a dedicated stand-alone system, a front-end mini-computer connected to a large host computer or a multiple mini-computer network system. A network of minicomputers allows a large library with many branches to build its own internal network. The minicomputers can be used for various library Operations: acquisition, cataloguing, database creation and maintenance, circulation control, serials control, information storage and retrieval, communication and networking and management works. Minicomputers have many advantages over large computers. They are smaller, cheaper, more reliable and do not require a carefully controlled operational environment.

Micro-computers and micro-processors have further enlarged the scope for the introduction of automation in library works. These machines can alto be used for acquisition, serials control, circulation, cataloguing, abstracting and indexing, on-line searching, data management systems, administration, communications and training. The rapid development of micro-computer technology and the resultant reduction in the price of computer machines have brought them within the means of many libraries in the developing countries. A major deterrent to widespread use of micro-computers in information handling activities is the lack of adequate software. Operating systems for micro-computers are under-developed compared to those available on mini-computers. At the present stage of development, software may cost much more than the system hardware. However, operating systems for micro-computers are becoming sophisticated, and there are indications of development of standard softwares for their effective use in libraries and information centres.

Computer in Indian Libraries

In India the number of computer installations has gone up considerably in recent years. Some of our important research and special libraries are reported to have introduced computerized services in the area of library housekeeping operations and/or information retrieval. The names of some of these institutions maybe cited here: Bhaba Atomic Research Centre (Bombay), Bharat Heavy Electrical Ltd (Hyderabad), Central Food and Technological Research Institute (Mysore), Indian Institute of Technology, Indian Standards Institution (Delhi), National Aeronautical Laboratory (Bangalore), Physical Research Laboratory (Ahmedabad), Tata Institute of Fundamental Research (Bombay), Indian National Scientific Documentation Centre (New Delhi), Documentation Research and Training Centre (Bangalore), Central Drug Research Institute (Lucknow), National Library (Calcutta). Most of these operational systems have been developed independently in different computer languages. The libraries have no say in the matter of choice of hardware and software; they have to make use of whatever facilities are available in their respective institutions. One system cannot be applied to another system, and if a new library wants to introduce automation it has to develop its own capabilities.

The current controversy centres round the adoption of a standardized software for computer communication among libraries. Some are in favour of the Common Communication Format (CCF) and some want the Machine Readable Catalogue (MARC) format. The controversy has arisen in the context of the establishment of local library networks like Delhi Library Network (DELNET) and

Calcutta Library Network (CALIBNET). It has, however, been learnt that there is scope of conversion from one format to another. In this connection the UNESCO developed user-friendly library software package CDS/ISIS may be mentioned. It is being distributed free of cost to the libraries with computer facilities by NISAT in the Department of Science of Technology, Government of India. INSDOC has started regular courses for computer application in libraries. It is also being included by some universities in post-graduate library science courses. If the present trend continues all important libraries of the country may be computerized by the end of the century.

Important Features

1. Use of main-frame, mini and micro-computers with large memory capabilities should be introduced and supported in major libraries of the country;
2. Priority should be given to development of application software packages for library and information activities for use in indigenously manufactured computer system;
3. Use of communication facilities for developing inexpensive local library and information networks has to be supported for practicing resource-sharing. These local library and information networks can be utilized for evolving national library and information network;
4. Low-cost copying services through provision of reprography and micrography facilities should be available in major libraries so that document back-up could be provided;
5. Compaction of library and information material by means of microform media, magnetic tapes, video discs, and so on should be encouraged in the context of saving storage space;
6. Provision for mobile audio-visual information in Indian languages should be made for rural areas to serve neo-literates, post-literates, students of open universities, and so on as a supplement to national TV network.
7. On line facilities through national data communication networks should be evolved in order to provide for interactive use of locally generated databases as well as to have access to international information network;

8. New technologies like videotex and teletext provide ample opportunities for disseminating information quickly and effectively. Such systems should be experimented with a view to studying their impact on the society and on the mechanism of their introduction.

7

Computers in Information Storage

How to Access Information

Information is stored and preserved only for the purpose of making it available whenever and wherever that is needed. Even if all the information is kept in recorded form, its availability cannot be ensured to the needy. To a considerable level availability requirements are realized by libraries throughout the world. But no single library or a group of libraries currently may not serve the information needs of all. To get any information, first of all one should know where that information is available in what form it is and how it can be obtained. Even in getting this information about information, many libraries may not be able to help their users because of various practical difficulties. In fact, providing information about information is an aspect of management and control of information. The control and management of information is becoming more and more difficult with the exponential growth of volume of information.

Contemporary Society has been experiencing an ever increasing growth of information. A general estimate of this growth may be put a the current rate of 250 million words per hour if recorded. Each library gets, or is at least expected to get, a considerable share of this wealth. With this unusual growth of information, with its variety and abundance, it has become impractical, if not impossible, to ascertain by traditional methods what information exists, and where and how they can be obtained.

Information Management using Computer

Computer is meaningfully called an Information Processing Machine or even a Symbol Processing machine indicating that it is a machine for processing information formed by symbols. Symbols are the alphabets and special characters used in a natural language like English. All computers process information formed by the symbols of the English language. And we know that any information can be recorded in English. This leads us to the conclusion that any information can be processed using a computer. By processing we mean any conversion of information, from one symbolic form to another including a form in which you see information on paper to a form in which the computer records it and then back to the original form.

Computer Functions in Libraries

To examine how computer does the information processing activity, let us make a small computer, generally called a personal computer, as an example. For such a computer, there s a typewriter like keyboard with all the symbols we use in English. Using this keyboard, also called an input device, we can feed information to the computer in the form of symbols. Some piece of information can be considered to the COMMANDS to the computer asking it to do something for you. In fact computer is a machine made to work according to symbolic commands given to it. Now think of a command to ask the computer to store whatever information you are feeding to it through the keyboard after giving the command. The computer can accept such a command and store for you the information you are feeding. You know that the computer stores the information in a part of it called its memory. And the stored information we want to get back for use. Since we are likely to use information in various forms for different purposes, we want to keep it separately in a distinguishable form. Manually we do it made to do likewise. So we can ask the computer to kept information in FILEs so that we can we distinguish it and use effectively.

The memory of the computer mentioned above is having some limitations. First of all, this memory is active only when the computer is ON. On failure of electricity the information stored in memory will be lost. Hence, we cannot store information stored in memory will be lost. Hence, we cannot stored information permanently in this memory. Secondly, this memory is very much limited in capacity when we think of storage of large volume of information. To meet these two drawbacks, a computer is always provided with some form of Auxiliary or Secondary memory on some medium, equivalent to the paper medium for human where the computer can store information in a nondestructive or permanent form. Several such media are available for computers. The most commonly used for the personal computer is called a Floppy Disk. The usual variety of it has a diameter of 5.25 inches and is encased in a protective cover of square shape. With the protective cover, its thickness is only one and a half millimeter. A variety of this small diskette is capable of holding 12 lakhs symbols on it. It is similar to a music record. On a music record what is recorded is sound, on a floppy disk what is recorded are symbols.

How information can be recorded on to such a diskette? We have seen that we can feed information into the memory of the computer. At any moment, we can ask the computer to copy the information it is holding in its memory on to a diskette attached to the computer. And once it is done, that much information which is stored on to the diskette remains permanently stored. After this you can go on adding information to the memory and occasionally store it on to the diskette. When one diskette becomes full, you can replace it with another on. Thus any volume of information can be recorded on diskettes using personal computer.

Information record on diskettes is not directly readable to human beings. To access that information you need a computer, exactly as you needed one to record information on to diskettes. You can ask a computer to read the information (kept in a FILE) on a diskette into its memory and give you back from there. But where it will give this information? It has to produce it on some medium in symbolic form.

Thus in the functioning of a computer we distinguish the following units: an input device to give information to the computer, a memory unit where the computer holds information temporarily, a unit which helps the computer store information permanently on medium like floppy disk and units like display screen and printer through which the computer gives you information back after processing. We can think of one more unit of the computer which controls all the activities of the computer and does all the processing on information given to it. Let us call it the Central Processing Unit. All these constitute the basic functional units of a computer.

Storage Method

One main consideration for storage of information is compactness. Especially in a library environment, this is very important. Compactness of information can save a lot of storage space and facilitate easy handling. For example, a library with one lakh holdings can store all the information about then (with 500 characters for each) in 42 floppy diskettes of the type we have seen earlier.

Let us see some media other than the floppy diskette we have seen. Diskettes of the same size with lesser capacities are also widely used. Those with 362,000 characters and 724,000 characters capacities are examples. There is another type of floppy disk smaller in size measuring three and a half inches in diameter, but large in capacity. Optical diskettes of twelve centimeters in diameter, also called Compact Disk, are now offering upto 650 million characters capacity. That means, one such diskette can hold deaths of 13 lakhs documents.

Other than these, disk packs consisting of several diskettes packed together have been in use with computers. Their capacities vary from twenty million characters to six thousands million characters per pack.

Like diskettes, there are several types of tapes in cassettes used as medium for information storage by computer. Cassette tapes of 40 million, 60 million and 150 million characters capacity are now in use. Prospects of availability of compact tapes of a thousand million characters capacity are bright.

Diskettes and cassette tapes are comparatively new in the field of computer storage media. They all came with small computers. But prior to that several types of larger tapes and disks were in use with large computers. New varieties of them with larger and larger capacities have been coming into use regularly for example, a magnetic tape of half inch width presently in use can hold upto eight thousands characters per inch of length. The length of one tape spool is usually 2400 feet with lesser ones in length optionally available. Large disk packs capable of holding more than two thousands million characters are now in common use. Special type of storage device called Mass Storage Devices capable of providing 472 Billion characters storage are also used with some large computer. As mentioned earlier, it should be remembered that a large computer can have dozens of high capacity storage units providing for tapes and disks attached to it. In short, the storage that can be made available with a computer can be enormous to meet any demand.

Computer Operations

Now, being convinced that ample storage can be made available with the computer to meet any information storage need, let us come back to the method of feeding information to the computer. Whatever we do on the computer, we have seen that it is done through giving commands to the computer. There are dozens of commands that can be given to the computer at various levels of usage. At the highest level, you can command the computer at the level of the Operating System which is a larger set of programs supplied along with the computer when one is acquired, and which makes the computer usable to the large majority of computer users. Under the control of the Operating System, facilities for storage and retrieval of information can be requested through commands. For example, through commands, you can create an empty file and go on adding and correcting (if needed) information in the file. You can store the file on to a disk, or make another copy of the file, all through commands. For adding information to the file, you can get facilities to structure the information into different parts; for example, let us call the 500 characters long information about a document as a record and think of it in terms of various parts like a Number Field, Classification field, Author Field, Title Field, etc. Information regarding a document can be entered part by part conveniently, without confusion, with the help of commands.

Information Retrieval

After storing a large volume of information, let us now think of using it. On the usage part, we are generally selective. In a particular Information Retrieval requirement, what we need may be a set of documents recently published on a very narrow and specific field.

In such a retrieval problem, to get information about say a dozen documents, million of records may have to be searched. This is definitely impossible for a human being to accomplish in a short time, even in a few days. But a computer may do the job in a few minutes, if not in seconds. It can be programmed to search through all the records stored and made available to the computer and give you the list of documents in minutes or seconds. By programme, we mean by giving the computer a sequence of instructions in a specific order. These instructions will ask the computer to copy a larger block of records from the disk to the memory, go through them to find out whether any record satisfying our requirements are there, if yes to print them, if not to bring in the next block from disk, and to continue till all the records in the data base are searched through. The computer will do this job at an unbelievably fast speed.

The instructions of constituting a problem can be prepared in any of a large collections of computer programming language. Of course with each computer, the set of languages that can be used to write programs for it is limited. The complexity in writing programs will vary from language to language. Fortunately very simple languages are now available making the use of computers requiring no special skill. There are special languages and language like package exclusively for use in computer applications in libraries.

On-Line Sharing

Currently, it is impractical for any library to keep an exhaustive collection of all the publication world-wide, not even those available in a country, or to have information on the availability of all the information. This problem can only be solved through the sharing of information between various libraries. By this we mean making available information at a place to another point where it is not available. This is effectively done by connecting computer network. In such a network, information in any of the connected computers can be made available to users of all the computers in the network. Thousands of users can be connected to this network through simple communication terminals thus making a large volume of information available to them. Now there are several such computer networks making world-wide online bibliographic services a reality.

Conclusion

Online bibliographic services are the ultimate answer to problems of information dissemination. The availability of this service alone make it accessible to the needy. A major deterrent factor is the communication cost involved. Increasing the number of users may bring down the cost. The growth of awareness of the conveniences offered by computer technology and the fast developments in the field may offer better solutions. Better control, higher productivity, improved efficiency, extended information services, etc. are the approved and accepted qualities attributed to computers in the service of information management.

MODERNISATION OF UNIVERSITY AND COLLEGE LIBRARIES IN INDIA: NEW CHALLENGES

Overview

There has been during the 1980s a growing interest in and concern over modernisation of library operations and services in India. The number of seminars, discussions and publications that this country had in this decade on this subject substantiates this observation. Special mention needs to be made here about the 33rd All India Library Conference which had as its theme 'Modernisation in Libraries', held at Tiruchirapalli in December 1987. Recently there was held in the University of Mysore a National Seminar on Modernisation of Library Service in University Libraries. Professional Library Associations and Library and Information Science teaching departments/institutions have, from time to time, conducted specialized training programmes for working librarians, in computer application. Particular reference may be made here to the series of short-term courses conducted by the D. R. T.C., Bangalore and other under the NISSAT Manpower Training programme. The Advanced Level Institute for Library conduced by the Kerala University Department of Library and Information Science during May-June 1987 was an occasion for Library Science teachers in many of the Indian universities in acquiring both theoretical and practical grip over the task of library computerization so that they could teach the subject later with greater confidence.

Modernisation of Libraries

Library modernization is often misunderstood in India as library computerization, although the concept does not contain computerization as its essential component. Modernization may include computerization as may be some other forms of information technology. There can be modernization even without computerization. Modernization is a relative concept, its relativity being to the existing stat-of-the-art in a given context. The state-of-the-art in library operations and services may be widely different from country to country, and even within the same country from library to library. Generally, speaking, libraries in the developed countries have been using many of the recent advances in the field of information technology, communication technology and micrographics, libraries in most of the less developed countries are still continuing with their traditional library operations and services that are mainly manual and non-mechanized.

Modernization, mainly, signifies an attitude of mind towards changing value. As Paul Wasserman wrote: "We live in a society whose only constant may be change... Change has been characteristic of human condition. What is different at present is the pace of change. Since we are in a fast changing society that our institutions should respond to the changes is crucial to their continued relevance. Library as a social institution is not an exception to this general rule. Librarian has to perceive the socio-cultural changes that are taking place around him and work out appropriate strategies for adjusting the organizational forms to the pace of change. Not to do so would be inviting an eventual degradation and disrepute for his profession.

Need for Library Modernisation

There are both global and national perspectives in modernization of libraries. At the global level substantial amount of work has been already turned out in designing and implementing strategic plans for modernizing libraries and information system. International organizations like UNESCO, the FID, and the IFLA have been constantly working for a New International Information Order wherein there will be the unimpeded, smooth and speedy flow of information among nations and individuals. The UNISIST programme for a global information system and the NATS programme for its national components, have provided the library world with basic guidelines regarding the scope and extent of modernization possible and desirable in the changing world order.

National perspective have been in conformity with the above global perspective. During the last two decades, practically, every country has been working at its national component of the proposed world information system. In some of the developed countries the progress made in this direction has been both astonishing and enviable.

(i) that information is the most crucial resource for development, and those who have better information are always in an advantageous position compared to others;

(ii) that development and utilization of the information resources are increasingly dependent upon the development and application of information and communication technologies; and

(iii) that the information advantage in development is dependent upon the information accessing and utilizing capability of the individual citizens.

It is the timely realization of the crucial role of information as a development factor that has led developed countries of today to their present position. An evident phenomenon of the development scenario of today is that the "information-rich" are also the developed countries, while the "information-poor" are also those remaining undeveloped, U. S. A., Soviet Union, Japan, Federal Republic of Germany, U. K. and France are among countries who recognized the value of information early enough and built up necessary infrastructure to harness it for optimal utilization in every field. They are today economically, industrially, scientifically and technologically the most advanced and also affluent countries.

Information Technology

Among conditions that favour library modernization the most significant has been the advent of the new information technology, a factor which even shaped both the global and national perspectives. The technologies possibilities that are opened up now for harnessing information through application of certain revolutionary developments in areas like micro-electronics, satellite communication, micrographics, compact discs, fibre optics, etc. have made the concept of the global information system an attainable target. Although our country has not had such a degree of development in these areas as in the case with developed nations of the world what we have attained so far are commendable particularly in the field of tele-communication. Our major cities have international dialing facilities, while STD facilities are available in most of our towns. Electronic Mail service has recently connected 7 cities in India, namely, Delhi, Bombay, Calcutta, Madras, Bangalore, Hyderabad and Port Blair.

Already on-line facility to access international databases has been made use of by some organizations atleast through the interface of telex or microcomputers. Recently, the American Cultural Centre Library at New Delhi, is reported to have established on-line facility to access DIALOG (California) database through telecommunication line to Hong Kong and the packet-switched system from there to DIALOG. Another significant development in this line has been the opening of an International Gateway in Bombay to international databases known as the Gateway Packet Switching Service (GPSS) by the Videsh Sanchar Nigam Limited (VSNL). This has brought down the cost of on-line searching substantially.

New technologies have opened up cost-saving possibilities for individual libraries also. The closing years of the 1980s witnessed almost a microcomputer boom. Five years ago an Indian PC with a minimum configuration cost more than a lakh of rupees. But, by 1989 this price has come down to Rs. 25,000. Now, the people's PC brought out by the ET & T costs only around Rs. 11,000. The Indian Information Technology industry has crossed the mark of Rs. 1000 crores during the year 1989-89. Noticeable trends in the microcomputer technology are higher clock speeds and storage capacities the Intel 80286 chip with 8-12 MHz has been replaced by the 80386-based super PC/AT in 1987, and the 80486 is already in the market. PCs are now overtaking mainframes and minies in library applications. Software availability also does not pose any serious problems. Several Computer manufactures and software houses are marketing library and information oriented packages. UGC has found not less than 162 such software package, of various capabilities, in India, although only a few of them are meant for integrated library operations. The application package available for integrated library operations like the MINISIS (for a multiuser environment with a mini-computer) and the CDS/ISIS microversion (for single-user environment) are definitely plus points. The CDS/ISIS is available/free of cost to educational and scientific institutions. Although CDS/ISIS is made for a single user environment with MS-DOS as the Operating System, it can be worked also in a LAN environment with multi-user facilities.

State of Art Indian Scenario

The state-of-the-art in library operations and services obtainable in India, especially in the University and college libraries, by and large, can be called traditional. There has been impressive growth in collection, services and personnel in university libraries during the past four decades, due mainly to the financial support given by the University Grants Commission. Nevertheless, it remains a sad fact that our university libraries have not been able to create the desired impact on the academic community. Libraries are still passive appendages to colleges and universities. They could not be integrated with the teaching and learning process. Librarians having acquired parity in status and emoluments with the academic staff get lost in route jobs, mostly deskworks. The classification and cataloguing have become complex and cumbersome jobs. The open access system is cracking down to chaos. Losses, mishandling and mutilation of books are on the increase. Pre-occupation with deskworks prevent the library staff from having proper interaction with readers.

Our university libraries are far behind their counter parts in other countries in the matter of the utilization of modern information technology. The collections are almost solely in printed books and periodicals. The multi-media and non-print records have yet to make their entry into university libraries. During the last two decades there has been some response to the advent of new information technology. Some libraries have gone for microfilm readers and photocopying machines. But in several cases these are prestigious possessions that are not allowed to be adequately used by readers. There are libraries who have acquired microcomputers without considering the compatibility of operating systems to software packages.

Outside the university and college libraries, library automation activities are going on in a number of institutions in India. Special mention may be made here of the Bhabha Atomic Research Centre, Bombay, Tata Institute of Fundamental Research, Bombay, Physical Research Centre, Bombay, Physical Research Laboratory, Ahmedabad, Indira Gandhi Centre for Atomic Research, Kalpakkam, Steel Authority of India Ltd., Ranchi, Bharat Heavy Electricals Ltd., Hyderabad, and National Informatics Centre, New Delhi. In the area of computerization of bibliographic information processing a number of projects are being worked on by organization in India like the INSDOC, BARC, DRTC, the Electronics Commission, Physical Research Laboratory, NIC, etc.

The scenario described above is conspicuous for lack of standardization and co-ordination. Modernization of library and information systems and services cannot be taken up haphazard and governed by curiosity or prestige motives. It should be properly planned and implemented on the basis of good system studies. Modernization is not just the introduction of new machineries and equipments, it must include modernization of men, materials and services.

Information Education

Modernization of libraries has to be seen from two different angles: the angle of the information providers (librarians), and the angle of the information users. Both information use and information provision are inter-related activities, one influencing the other. We know that information users' needs, patterns and behaviour can change the pattern of information provision. But, we must also know that new patterns of information organization and provision can lead to new information needs and use patterns and behaviour. In our traditional library set-up the reader is used to the age old practice of looking for documents through the catalogue or open access to shelves where his expectations are based on mostly some prior information about specific documents can be incomplete or outdated. Or the documents he is looking for may not be available there on the shelf. Further, his chance for exposures of other useful documents, or "accidental discoveries", on the open shelves is often constrained by limitations of time and environment. These and other reasons may discourge him from using the library to the desired extent. On the other hand, computerized catalogues and bibliographical database can make the reader's search for information and documents more interesting and rewarding, and accessing them speedier and more comprehensive.

The availability of an inexpensive photocopying service in the library will be an essential facility in fulfillment of the requirements of the Fourth Law of Library Science, "Save the time of the Reader." In the absence of this, if a reader is tempted to cut out the relevant pages from the library book or periodical, it cannot be just adjudged as an unsocial act. Modern information technology can provide satisfactory solutions to many such behavioral problems among the changing generation of readers.

Libraries have to modernize their operations and services in such a way as to encourage and promote the information capability of its readers. Assuming that information is available and accessible, the user must have the ability to search, locate and use it. This is the information capability of the user. Libraries can develop information capability in readers through proper user education programmes. Then only, modernization of libraries can open up the benefits of the new information technology to our user communities.

The INFLIBNET Programme

Modernisation of libraries in India as a subject and attracted the attention of many national bodies and professional organisations during the last two decades. But the most recent and relevant document dealing with modernisation of university library operations and services in India is the Report of the Inter Agency Working Group of the University Grants Commission on the Development of an Information and Library Network to be called the INFLIBNET. The document sets out a project proposal for the establishment and development of the above named network in the country during the VII Five Year Plan (1990-95) period. The Government of India has accepted this proposal for implementation. This proposal has emerged as a logical consequence of the new national Policy on Education, 1986 and the National Policy on Library and Information Systems, 1986. It has also taken into account the overall aims and objectives of the national policies on science and technology and the recommendations made by some of the Government bodies concerned with science and education from time to time. Special mention needs to be made here about the Report of the Steering Group on Science and Technology and Environment, and the Report of the Planning Commission Working Group on Modernisation of Library Services and Informatics, both being in the context of the Seventh Five Year Plan (1985-90). Both these reports have emphasised the need for computerisation of libraries while the latter has even proposed the development of a computer network interlinking all special libraries in India by 2000 A.D.

Taking into account these and other proposals the University Grants Commission, as the national body directly concerned with higher education, constituted in April 1988 a Committee on National Network System for Universities and Colleges under the chairmanship of Prof. Yash Pal, the Chairman of the UGC.

Outlook

INFLIBNET is designed as a computer-communication network of libraries and information centres using satellite-cum-terrestrial networking. It would link up the institutions of higher learning covering all disciplines and all major R & D institutions and national level organisations. It will operate at different levels-national, regional, sectoral and local. The overall structure of the INFLIBNET can be outlined as follows:

There will be:

(i) a National Centre for managing, overseeing and co-ordinating the affairs of the network;

(ii) four Regional Centres (North, East, West, and South) each of which will maintain Regional Union Catalogues and Databases of projects, institutioins, and specialists;

(iii) as many Sectoral Information Centres comprising the 4 UGC Information Centre (in Sciences, Social Sciences, Humanities, and Engineering), and the 7 Sectoral Information Centres of the NISSAT, and other national level information centres, like the NML, DESIDOC, IARI, etc. These Sectoral Information Centres will acquire, create and access both retrospective and current bibliographic databases including the international databases available on magnetic tapes, databases of projects, institutions and specialists; and

(iv) 100 Document Resource Centres designated from among university and R & D institutional libraries.

The management of the INFLIBNET will rest with a registered society to be constituted for the purpose. The project is expected to be completed in a period of 4 years (from April 1990 to March 1994).

Functions and Services

INFLIBNET is a multiple function/service network. functions/services are:

1. Catalogue-based service – including shared cataloguing; union catalogue, on-line catalogue access, and catalogue production in card, book, magnetic tape/floppy, CD-ROM, and COM form;
2. Data base service – including bibliographic data base services for restrospective search, SDi and CAS, and non-bibliographic database services like information on-going and completed projects, institutions, and specialists;
3. Documents supply services – including inter-library loan, and documnet delivery through FAX and non-FAX (like Xerox copies microfilm/microfiche, etc);

The project report of INFLIBNET is a complete document covering all aspects like the background and objectives, output and services and their organisation, standardization for information handling, application software requirements, computer hardware specifications, network communication architecture, data capturing and preparationi, manpower training, management mechanism, implementation mechanism, and cost implications.

INFLIBNET in University Libraries

According to the UGC-INFLIBNET proposal the university libraries in India have a very crucial role to play. Fvery large university library will have to function either as one of the 100 Document Resource Centres to be designated, or as the seat of one of the 150 Ground Terminals, or both. Being the Ground Terminal the university library will be the centre catering to all the local needs in the Local Area Network including department libraries and college libraries through its interface to the Regional Information Centre. However, the primary task before the university library will be the compilation of the union catalogue of the libraries under its purivew. The INFLIBNET project proposes to aggregate the catalogues of libraries bottom-upwards, ie. from the college libraries and the departmental libraries to the university library, and from the university libraries in a region to the Regional Information Centre. It is estimated that there will be about 9 million unique catalogue records of the retrospective collections of the 179 university libraries in the country. These have to be converted and unified into a common catalogue database according to the prescribed standard. A part of this work is proposed to be done by matching the catalogue records with those available from down-loaded imported tapes such as of LC-MARCH, OCLC, and WLN.

INFLIBNET will provide adequate funds to meet all the cost of hardware, software, and humanware. For this purpose, the university libraries are grouped into three according to their size. The large libraries are those having a collection over 3,00,00 volumes. The Medium size libraries are those having between 100,000 and 300,000 volumes. The small libraries are those having less than 100,000 volumes.

INFLIBNET in Kerala

INFLIBNET is a major national effort to improve the information capability of the nation through modernisation of libraries and information systems. Its success depends upon the whole-hearted co-operation of the library profession. The university librarians, particularly, must take this as a challenge and come out with concrete proposals as to how best their share of work in the overall national endeavour could be organised and accomplished as per the time schedule. It is equally a challenge for library schools who have to train the personnel for working with the new system, and who also have the teachers with the required expertise in many of the matters connected with the modernisation of library operations and services.

(i) The Trivandrum Area Library Network,
(ii) The Kottayam Area Library Network,
(iii) The Cochin Area Library Network,
(iv) The Trichur Area Library Network,
(v) The Calicut Area Library Network.

Each of the above 5 networks can be developed by taking each of the 5 universities in Kerala as the focal point. Each university library will aggregate the catalogues of the departmental libraries, and the college libraries in its area with its own catalogue to form the union catalogue for the Area. According to the INFLIBNET plan, there will be three Ground Terminals in Kerala connecting the local networks to the national network through satellite. These three Ground Terminals are now proposed as one for Trivandrum, one for Kottayam and Cochin together, and one for Trichur and Calicut together. The union catalogue data from all the 5 areas can be aggregated through the Ground Terminals into the Regional Union Catalogue of the Southern Region.

The Kerala State Library Network needs to be planned and developed as a multi-type library network. This will be in conformity with the recent national policy proposals and recommendations besides satisfying the requirements of the INFLIBNET. Special reference may be made here to the recommendation of the Empowered Committee under chairmanship of Prof. D.P. Chattopadhyaya which was appointed by the Department of Culture, Government of India in 1986 to propose a programme of action for implementing the National Policy on Library and Information Systems. This Committee has recommended that all public libraries within a State should form part of an information database network, and that resource sharing of universities, colleges and research organisations in a region/State should be facilitated through linkage and network.

ECONOMICS OF COMPUTERISATION IN INDIAN LIBRARIES

Overview

The driving force behind an information revolution is computer. It is one of the most powerful forces in society today. It is being put to use everywhere, it seems—in homes and in organisations of all nature and sizes—and none can doubt that this usage is having a stronger impact on many people. Since the 1960s libraries have used technology in general and computers in particular, to automate a wide range of administrative, public and technical service tasks. It has become the librarian's status symbol. To admit to working in a library which is not computerised is to imply that your place of employment is small or backward; and such an admission is usually hastily qualified by the explanation that computerisation is being considered. Certainly those who put their faith in something other than electronics are in danger of being regarded as deviants.

Library automation is a major undertaking which requires a positive operational justification, an examination of the pros and cons and a realisation that it will, in the course of time, change the whole nature and approach of the library. Whether that change will be for the better or worse will depend on 3 things:

(i) how the introduction of computer was undertaken;

(ii) how realistic were the objectives in library terms; and

(iii) how reasonable were the original projections of what could be accomplished by the use of the computer.

Economics of Computerisation

The subject scope of this article deals with the final question which is with regard to the economics of computerisation discussed with reference to Indian libraries. "Economics" can be defined by both its subject matter and its approach. Although people tend to think of economics in connection with buying and selling, its subject, more generally is "Choices": the allocation of resources among the competing ends. Economics can be and has been applied to virtually every sphere of human behaviour. The essence of economic approach is its assumptionis; (i) that people generally behave rationally to maximise their utility or wellbeing; and (ii) that they compare costs and benefits and allocate their resources, including time and money, to achieve their goal. This description of the economic approach, of course, is an extreme simplification. Becker and Mackenzie have described the economic approach at greater length.

Two major research areas are subsumed to by the term "economics of library automation/computerisation."

Economics of Computerisation: Indian Scenario

The Indian scenario today presents a strange spectrum of contradictions: few libraries being totally automated in the absence and failure of producing even the current, and uptodate national bibliography. Adoption is not important but participaion is that which counts. Thus, while computerisation might have come into India in the 'Chronological sense' or in the 'literal sense', but not in the evaluation sense of the thrm, that is, not in the sense that there is a change in the outlook of the people, or in the system of ideas. As a matter of fact, the ideas and the fruits of computerisation have accured to only a marginal fringe of the total population, leaving a vast majority of tem gaping in wonder and disbelief. This is the root cause of the trap in which the Indian society finds itself today eager to change, but powerless to do so. This leads us to only one conclusion – libraires in India cannot be computerised so long as the Indian society itself is not ready to change. They are so deep-rooted in conventioned techniques and methods, that it is hard for them to witch over to modern way in a spurt.

An important topic within the economics of libraries is the cost-benefit study. Cost-benefit and cost-effectiveness analysis are methods of comparing the costs and benefits of altenatives. The difference between them is the measure of value or benefit used and the uses to which such methods can be put. Cost-effectiveness is less general than cost-benefit, and can only be used for resource allocation decisions within the library. Cost-benefit analysis can be used to compare library service with other activities. Cost-effectiveness express the results or value of the activity in measures of effectiveness. Cost-effectiveness can only be used to compare alternatives that have the same objectives. For example, cost-effectiveness measures can be used to compare different methods of providing the same library service. Many studies have measured the costs of library services and function. The usefulness of these studies is that their methods can be translated to other situations. The results of cost-effectiveness studies generally studied. Hence, its major short coming is its inability to place relative values on the benefits to different groups. Raffel notes that this where economic analysis gives way to political analysis as he cannot tell how to equate different group's differences.

(i) Material (Availablility of computer hardware and software)

(ii) Finance

(iii) Manpower

These three factors are measured against its effectiveness and benefit in the Indian context.

In India we have not been able to capitalise the utility of computers compared to westernc ountries such as indigenous development of chips, import restriction and prices. However, there is an increasing awareness among the people about the utility of computers and the anticipated price reduction of the computers in the coming years. What we need is the government support to build suitable infrastructure and create the manufacturing facility in the country to take advantage of this important piece of equipment for solving enormous problems.

Computers, micro-processors and other gadgets of information technology are found to be used to some extent in scientific libraries in India. There seems to be very little efforts in the direction of introducing the computers in public libraries; and this, however, cannot be said anymore with reference to academic libaries lack in the basic requirements like separate building, sufficient space, furniture, reading materials other than the conventional book form, even that which is insufficient maintenance and above all staff. In the absence of all these minimal and fundamental pre-requisites, it is a wonder to note the fire of 'computer culture' amongst us. Ofcourse, computers are versatile fools in terms of efficiency economy and maintaureability. Undoubted by with the availability of minicomputers and the decline of their prices, their use of house-keeping operations and services to users in libraries is relevant today. So library can nowadays services in a global economy with obsoloscent facilities. "In a developing country like ours it is in our own interest to accept and adapt to the new changes and to devise the best way and means to benefit from the new revolutionary technologies. If we ignore it, we will find ourselves relatively speaking back in the stone age. "Our competitive edge in low labour costs is already being wiped out and unless we adapt our systems to computerisation, use will find world market for our products evaporate fast."

Till 1982, the big deterent to the introduction of computers in libraries was their cost. It was beyond the reach of majority of libraries to spend so huge amounts in the purchase of mainframes and mini-computers. However, micro-computers have come as a big relief as they were much cheaper. There are about 50 organisations in India which are manufacturing hardware and the annual turnover is about 5000 computer systems. The leading manufacturers,

International computers India Manufacturer Ltd, Bombay (ICIM) are manufacturing ICIM Business pc; Hindustan Computers Ltd, New Delhi (HCL Computers); Usha Micro-process Controls, New Delhi undertake the tradename Usha Computers; Blue Star, New Delhi market GP/5000 series 37 (Packard) computers; WIPRO Information Technology Ltd, Bombay (Wipro Series) and so on. In addition to these indigenous manufacturers, there are about 370 agents/dealers of foreign organisations in computer hardware. Regarding Software, there are about 165 software packages available in India, out of which 7-10 are exclusively meant for library operations. This trend reveals the accelerating process of technological innovation and the wider choice of computer hardware and software equipments at affordable prices within India itself. What is to be noted, inspite of this fact, the acquisition and installation of computer system is at lower rate functionally.

(i) Whether the entire system needs to be totally computerised at one stage;

(ii) Whether to partly computerise by identification and computerisation of functions which do no dislocate the normal working of the library; and

(iii) Whether to run 2 systems parallel to each other till the computerisation is complete.

The choice of any one of the above depends upon the need for one such changeover in a particular library, and its financial position. There are few special libraries where entire system is totally computerised as they could afford it and is well enjoy management's and user's appreciation and satisfaction. As regards the Academic libraries, Scenario in India it is yet to reach a long distance. Even the second phase of partly being computerised in chosen areas of library activities is not seen to be much taken upt. To run the third phase-2 parallel system-is beyond scope because of its enormous cost. As for the public libraries, neither the government nor the public are computer conscious and are prepared for such turn over. Above all, the impeding factor is poor budgeting. While the possibilities of the cheap computers are very exciting, in course of time, one can also envisage some of the imposing economic threats. Regarding its maintenance it is to be remembered that once the piper starts playing, he must be paid, continued to be paid. It seems that library field is too small a market to attract large investments to ensure purpose-built software for library activities.

(i) Increased and monotonous workload of library routine and repetitive operations;

(ii) Introdction of new services;

(iii) Need for co-operation and centralisation;

(iv) Need for increased speed of access and process;

(v) Need for preservation and storage;

(vi) Need to interact with international information systems all of which are totally computer-based.

These causes justify the efforts, cost and fine that need to be spent over the computerisation of libraries. What shall we the right effort. One test is that most often we obtain the derived result from it. We may, therefore judge, the effort by the fruit it yields.

To turn to the third resource is "Man Power'. By the term 'Manpower' is meant information workers. India is rich in manpower resource, who are available in abundane it all the three managerial levels-Top, middle and low. This surplus feature is not to be ignored while opting for computerisation. In spite of the many benefits we gain from computer usage, such usage also has potential problems and dangers. The significant one to be mentioned in this context is the employment problem.

Computer usage attaines produce displacement and unemployment-which are not the same. 'Unemployment' referes to the total number of people involutarily out of work., 'Displacement' occurs when technological change eliminates job. If displaced workers can't find similar jobs elsewhere or if they can't find other work, then there is, indeed, an increase in unemployment. And a significant displacement problem is accompanying the increased use of computer controlled system. However, more information is needed on the dynamics of the information labour market if libraries are to be sure to have qualified staff in inadequate numbers and librarians are to have jobs.

(i) ***Computers and Technology are an unflemished blessing:*** This uncritical optimistic view holds that technology is the course of all progress for people, that all socio-economic problems will inevitably be solved through the application of technology, and that every new technological possibility will automatically be beneficial.

(ii) ***Computers and Technology are an Unbridled Curse:*** This pessimistic view holds that technology increase unemployment, leads to depersonalisation, threatens our right to dignity and privacy, and threatens to polute or blow up the world.

(iii) ***Computers and Technology are underserving of Special attention:*** This unconcerned view holds that technology has been with us forever, and we are now better educated and more able than ever before to adopt to the changes which it has brought and will bring.

Conclusion

What is important about this line of research is its implications for libraries' future ability to maintain service levels without exponentially increasing budgets, and its evaluations of alternative actions that might be undertaken to stare off th disasters. It is not all clear whether libraries can expect increasing or static productivity with or without computers. Further research is needed into the internal and external factors that affect library productivity.

8

INFORMATION RETRIEVAL THROUGH COMPUTER IN LIBRARIES

Overview of Micro Computers

Remarkable development in computer technology has placed inexpensive computing power to desk top microcomputers. It is now possible for small libraries to computerise at least a few important functions of the library using a small-sized and low-priced desk top microcomputer supported with a suitable off-the-shelf general or specific purpose software package now available in a wide range. Besides the new policy of Government of India to promote use of computer technology in government and public sectors has made available a wide range of microcomputers with varied configurations. The micro has thus become a basic building block of library automation.

Software Development

The software development has gained a definite importance alongwith capabilities of microcomputers which have taken a quantum leap. Basically there are two types of software: packaged software and custom-designed software. The packaged software, available commercially, is pre-written, inexpensive and contains detailed documentation. The packaged software are generally user-friendly (`menu driven'), thus easy to use. The custom-designed software is designed by a programmer for use in a specific environment for a specific library. It is not only a time-consuming (`a pain-in-neck') activity but also an expensive one. More and more packaged softwares are now available for microcomputers with operating system such as MS-DOS and PC-DOS. Packaged softwares are written to take advantage of the facilities available under certain operating systems which, in turn, are configured to use certain hardware features. It is the programme, therefore, which dictates the way in which the computer operates and makes clear the capability of hardware, and thus should be chosen first. Once suitable software has been selected, it is possible to choose between the various makes of micros which support it. One can indeed accomplish many tasks with a micro if he has selected a right software coupled with right microcomputer. Selection and acquisition of a software package is a particularly difficult problem for the developing countries since.

Software Package

Some useful sources of information giving availability packaged software are as follows:

1. Burton, P. Microcomputer applications in libraries and information retrieval: A directory of users. Edinburgh; Leith Nautical College Library, 1981.
2. Ching-Chin Chen: Microuse directory: Software. West Newton, Masachusetts; Microuse Information, 1984.
3. Datapro directory of software. Buchillon; Switzerland; McGraw-Hill. (continuously updated reference source).
4. Gates, H. A directory of library and information retrieval software for microcomputers. Gower, 1984.
5. Gates, H. Library software for microcomputer. BLKJOD Report No. 5776. Oxford; Cains Library, John Redcliffe Hospital, 1983.
6. International directory of software 1983-84 (annual). London; Computer Publications Ltd., 1984.
7. Keren, C. and S.I. Sexed, ed. International inventory of software packages in the information field. Paris; Unesco, 1983. (UNISISTPGI/3/WS/28).
8. Nolan, J.M., ed. Micro software evaluation. Torrance, California; Nolan Information Management Services, 1984.

9. Software for text retrieval. Results of a survey conducted by the Southern Branch of the Institute of Information Scientists, 1983.
10. Vision Associates, ed. The CP/M software directory 1983 for professional microcomputers. Cambridge; Cambridge Information and Research Services Ltd., 1983.

Evaluation of a Software Package

Software package in general should match most of the criteria termed as a result of pre-assessed need of automation although users should be prepared to change their procedures where necessary to suit the requirements of package acquired. Since it may. not be possible either to provide full support for users from manufacturer of a software package or to tailor the package for specific individual requirements, Gates has enumerated following the criteria.

SIZE RESTRICTION

Package should be able to accommodate the maximum field, record, and files sizes required for operating the system.

DATA ENTRY

Inputting of data should be an easy operation specially when the amount of data entry is much. A formatted screen or prompts for the next field be preferable in such cases.

EDITING

Software package should provide for screen editing although editing may also be done by a compatible word processing package. UPDATE: Update procedure should be simple and fast.

CHANGING MODES

Input, edit, searching and printing are often separate modes. Package should allow faster means to change from one mode to another.

COMMANDS/MENU-DRIVEN

Menu-driven packages are easier to use than command driven packages specially for beginners.

HELP

Help facility should be elaborative and informative.

It may be helpful to test the system thoroughly. Contact with existing users and visit to existing installations can be a helpful guide. Besides, it should be seen that the vendor of software package should be committed for longterm support to their products and should have established reasonably consistent marketing policies. If a software is being bought for an existing hardware configuration, this is likely to be a main component of choice. The factors of price of software package alongwith its after-sale maintenance should also be considered.

Portable Software Development

Unesco's Second Medium-Term Plan (1984-1989) has laid emphasis on the development of portable software packages for free distribution to helpful member states in developing countries. These software will help to create databases which can handle locally produced information as well as facilitate the exchange of information in computer-readable form. Unesco's assistance to developing countries will also include the installation and maintenance of the appropriate software package, training in its use, and within the budgetary limits provision of the hardware as well. Member States that wish to establish mainframe or mini computer-based information systems can at present select from amongst a relatively large number of packages including CDS/ISIS or MINISIS (available free of cost to developing countries). Unesco has at present identified three software packages, IV + V System, Mini-Micro-CDS/ISIS and SUPERDOC.

Software Packages for Microcomputers and its Development

An Apple-IIe microcomputer with 64K main memory was procured at National Institute of Immunology (NII) mainly for word-processing purposes. The first author of this paper had then collected information regarding information storage and retrieval packages that can directly run on Apple-IIe. A software package called `Paperbase' was finally procured which can run directly on Apple-IIe. Here is some useful information on selective software packages based on practical experience with `Paperbase' software package. Some salient features of the three software packages, available free of cost from Unesco, are also given.

1. MINI-MICRO CDS/ISIS

This version of Unesco's CDS/ISIS package has been developed in collaboration with the Scuola Normale Superiore, in Pisa, Italy and is intended to implement all the functions of the mainframe version of the package while providing essentially the same operational characteristics to the user. A menu-driven additional interface is included in the package in addition to the normal CDS/ISIS commands which makes the training and use of the system simplified. The first version of mini-micro CDS/ISIS, operating in a multi-user environment on the Digital Equipment Corporation (DEC) PDP 11 Series of computer including microcomputer models of IBM PC-AT microcomputers, was available from mid-1985 to interested institutes in Member States which have signed the standard CDS/ISIS licence agreement. Request for details on this package should be addressed to Director of the Division of Library, Archives and Documentation Services, Unesco, Paris.

2. IV + V SYSTEM

High portability of IV+V is achieved by designing the system in such a fashion that the only interface of the software package with the hardware is at the level of P-code (Pseudo-code) interpreter (and not with operating system) which reacts directly with microprocessor as shown below:

IV + V SYSTEM

VCSD Pascal		P Code		Micro
Operating System	→	Interpreter	→	Processor

Portability is achieved by writing P-code interpreters for individual microprocessors. IV + V System is conceived as a generalised data base management system intended are both bibliographic and factual information management. Basic system functions are data entry, data editing, data base creation, and maintenance, retrieval and output. The system also includes screen processor which permits user-developed screens and user-controlled screen sequencing for specific applications and a task schedular which provides operating system control of tasks. IV + V is currently available for use on IBM PC-HT, IBM PC-AT, Wang PC and DEC Rainbow as well as on DEC-PDP 11 Series using the single user operating system. The package is available free of cost for non-profitable institutions in developing countries. Further information on the package may be obtained from Division of General Information, Unesco, Paris.

3. MicroCAIRS

It was developed from the CAIRS software package which has been functioning in many organisations in many western countries. MicroCAIRS has upword compatibilities with CAIRS enabling the users to switch from micro to mini/mainframe if the data base outgrows the capability of micro. The software can handle over 10,000 records (each around 500 characters long) on a IO M byte system. Records in a data base can be divided into SO sub files. Each record contains upto 80 fields with a maximum of 16,000 characters per record and a maximum of 2,000 characters per field.

MicroCAIRS allows the user to construct his own entry screen for online data entry. Records can be viewed, deleted or modified on-line once entered, using editing facility. The package supports both controlled or free language indexing as per the individual requirements. The package also offers an optional on-line thesaurus which assists users and regulates the selection of index key. MicroCAIRS provides for an elaborative search strategy using Boolean operators, combining sets, using truncation at either end or by using a thesaurus for broadening or narrowing terms. Besides, one can scan the inverted file or the thesaurus and determine term relationship. Search profile can be used to generate an SDI service which automatically performs searches against the latest additions to the data base.

4. LIBRARY MATE

Library Mate is a flexible information storage and retrieval package with limited capabilities. Each record can hold upto 700 characters. Approximately 125 of maximum size records will fit on a single disk. Each record can contain upto nine fields and the maximum length of any field is twenty five characters. One of those nine fields is designated as sort field. Each record can accommodate any number of keywords which can as well be code numbers. Search can be conducted by using Boolean combinations of keywords, if searches are to be done by one of fields like author, journal, name of publisher or date, then these items will have to be included as keywords. The package provides for several useful report formats. Records or portions of records with or without associated keywords can be listed with fields in any designated order. An index to keywords that cross-references record numbers can be produced as can be a dictionary of keywords. Alphabetical list of authors can be produced with cross references to record numbers. The package can run an Apple-IIe, Il or machines compatible with Apple system. The package sells for $ I79.95 and is available from Geosystems, Inc., 802E, Grand River, Williamson, MI 48895, USA.

5. BIBLIOTEK

Bibliotek is specially designed for inputting and retrieving bibliographic information and for producing printed bibliographies in a variety of formats, Bibliographic entries for books, periodical articles, and conference papers can only be entered in standard Bibliotek format. Upto ten authors can be entered per entry, but only initials are permitted and not full, first or middle names. Bibliotek programme automatically assigns punctuation and other style characteristics to each entry. Text editing functions are available. Title field and periodical or conference title is restricted to 240 characters and 128 characters respectively. Two Hundred character space is provided for entering comments or annotations. Fields for volume, pages, dates, etc. are also fixed in length. Users are required to develop a numbered keywords list or a numerical subject codes for keywords as the programme does not facilitate entry of complete keywords or subject headings. If additional keywords should be required after the initial list is developed, Bibliotek has provided a simple way to add them during the input of bibliographic entry. An alphabetically sorted list of keywords and their associated numbers can be produced on demand for reference while entering or retrieving items. Search routine using Boolean logic can search keywords or any character string in the record. Ultimate purpose of Bibliotek is to produce printed bibliographies.

6. SCI-MATE

Sci-Mate Version 1.1 consists of two components – the Personal Text Manager and the Universal Online Searcher. The off line component, the Personal Text Manager, is intended to accommodate bibliographic references, lab notes, correspondence, abstracts, and other forms of textual material. The Personal Text Manager has a variety of text-handling functions. One of IS major applications is as a reprint filing system. The reference storing file of Personal Text

Manager can store variable length records of upto 1900 characters. Menu-driven searches of stored records can be refined through Boolean logic. Truncation can also be used to allow stem searching. Bibliographic material, thus stored, can be flagged to indicate action taken, such as a reprint ordered or requested. Multiple-line report generator feature allows to print lists of authors, titles and other elements of record in a columnar format.

The online, component, the Universal Online Searcher, allows searching of data bases mounted on several large commercial vendors using a universal command language. The Universal Online Searcher will log on automatically. It will also automatically dial up the system if an automatic modem is used. Transferring information into Personal Text Manager from data bases that permit downloading allows the users to create their own data bases that are free-text searchable.

Online Searcher (now called Sci-Mate Searcher) and the Sci-Mate Editor. The Sci-Editor facilitate lay-out function of `Paperbase' beside many other editing functions which otherwise is being done using a word processing programme. Sci-Mate Version 2.0 has been designed for use on PC-DOS and MSDOE operating system. The package can run on CP/M operating system using a generic CP/M format. The package, thus, can be customized for APPLE, Kaypro, or DEC Rainbow computers, Sci-Mate Version 2.0 necessitate use of a hard disk since the Searcher, Manager and Editor all exceed the disk drive capacity of many microcomputers. Besides the generic CP/M version of Editor cannot be modified for use with APPLE. Because of size of the Editor programme and the limited memory of the APPLE precludes this: Cost (SciMate 1.1): Manager $ 540; Searcher $ 440; both together $ 880). The package is developed and sold by the Institute for Scientific Information, 3501, Market Street, Philadelphia, PA-19104, U.S.A.

7. REFED

REFED consists of five major routines. The main routine (also called REFED) allows the user to add, modify, search, sort, delete or save 2,000 reprints in a file. The REFLOAD routine converts references saved in files obtained from large data base (such as MEDLINE) to a form called `sequential text files' which can be read by other programmes such as word processors. REFPAGE allows the user to define page formats (printer codes, maximum number of lines per page, characters per line, margins, page number, etc.). REFPRINT may be used to print references using a variety of reference styles from which the user may choose or he may add his own (e.g. book format, Journal of Biological Chemistry format, etc.). The REFLOAD routine offers the opportunity to use three data bases (ESA-QUEST, DIALOG and ELHILL). The programme is said to be capable of saving 2000 references in a single file; to do so, the user must either have a hard disk drive or use a diskette with more storage capacity than the standard IBM PC double sided diskette. The software package is available for IBM PC compatible microcomputer and APPLE-II. REFED is available from Bio-soft, Sweden Violstigen 2, S-171 3 Salina, Sweden.

8. PAPERBASE

Paperbase, a minu-driven software package, is a suit of five programmes. STORE allows entry of references in standard Paperbase format of four lines (256 characters). The programme takes care of punctuation while prompting users for inputting data in a standard format. SEARCH reads through a file of references and lists up all that it contains on the topic of search, a keyword, year of publication, title, name of journal, or a combination of these fields. ORDER puts a list of references into alphabetical (or numerical) order. The alphabetising works by a straight character by character comparison between the first lines of references containing author's name and date of publication. LAYOUT rearranges references from the standard Paperbase format into any chosen format, e.g. for drawing up a reference list for a journal. HUNTER reads through the ASCII code fide and draws up a list of the probable citations it contains.

Paperbase software package, mainly aimed at information storage and retrieval needs of a scientist from his personal collection of reprints and other documents, is being used by first author of this article at National Institute of Immunology, New Delhi on APPLE-IIe microcomputer for information storage and retrieval. A double density 5¼" floppy stores about a thousand references. Search facility of the package was successfully tried to search by UDC numbers which were stored as keywords. UDC numbers can be stored as keywords because the programme stores all information as strings and does not differentiate between words and numbers. The original reprints, thus, can be filed by UDC numbers in filing cabinets. A provision is made to store abstracts on a separate floppy linked to references by giving a "key" in the 4th line of standard format denoting the abstract number. Paperbase offers a unique opportunity for an experienced programmer to modify the programme to meet unusual and individual needs. The programme can be freely copied. As far as an inexperienced user is concerned, unless he is able to buy a diskett version of the programme he will probably have to learn BASIC or hire a programmer who knows BASIC just to run the Paperbase. In nutshell, Paperbase is good information storage and retrieval package that can be improved upon.

Summary

The advantages of packaged software over custom-designed software are obvious. Users should be prepared to change their procedures where necessary to suit the requirements of software package acquired. There are numerous choices of software and hardware. Individual situation must be analysed in depth before making an attempt at exploring the market for selecting a set of hardware and software that will suffice the individual needs. In nutshell, sophisticated microcomputer technology now available along with a suitable software package allows a small library to attempt at automation at the same scale as does a mainframe computer to large libraries. Micro-version of software packages, earlier available only for mainframe or minicomputers (i.e. Mini-Micro CDS/ISIS, MicroCAIRS, MicroSTATUS etc.) should be put to use in Indian environment for automation of various functions of libraries. These packages have been tested through the passage of time and obviously have more capabilities than those attempted primarily for microcomputers. Unesco's programme for free distribution of software packages with back-up should be used by more and more libraries.

9

Serials Management through Computers

Introduction

A 1987 restructuring of the staffing pattern at the Stetson University Library resulted in the move of the faculty periodicals librarian position to a reference librarian position. The responsibility for periodicals was assigned to the head of the technical services department, a department which already included collection development, cataloging, and acquisitions. A technical assistant was hired periodicals supervisor to manage the day-to-day operations of a periodicals collection that included more than 47,000 bound volumes, 1,100 current subscriptions, and 1,300 inactive files. All of these titles were interfiled in one Kardex.

A project to buy microfiche in lieu of binding more than 350 titles had resulted in a large backlog of microfiche with no check-in system and inadequate financial control. More than one hundred new subscriptions were to be placed from a special endowment for the School of Business. The restructuring did not include more staff for serials, and it was clear that streamlining would be necessary.

The head of technical services (now associate director for technical services) began to explore the obvious answer of commercial serials control systems while making a study of serials vendors. As a result of the vendor study, EBSCO Subscription

Services was selected as the new agent. EBSCO installed an IBM PC/AT with a hard disk and a printer in the periodicals office, with a modem to connect to their central database. With the advantage of a personal computer conveniently located for the periodicals supervisor, we began to look for ways to meet immediate needs while deciding on a serials control system.

The head of technical services had experience with dBase III+ in developing an acquisition and fund accounting system. Although somewhat exacting, it is a flexible data management system as far as the range of reports and data manipulation that are possible. While the raw input screens in dBase can appear overwhelming, as they may include several display screens, the display and input patterns can be easily handled by creating screen formats. With these, the fields can be arranged in any pattern on the screen, and special identifiers for each field can prompt the person inputting the information.

By creating screen formats, using dBase .fmt files, each display screen can include fields that otherwise require four or more screens for display. dBase III+'s Assist function allows even the novice to "write" a program defining such formats, and function keys can be programmed as macros to reduce repetitive typing and input errors. With these evident advantages, dBase III+ was the logical choice for our serials management.

EBSCO: How to Work?

It is vital for this procedure that all fields in the receiving dBase file be in the same order and of the same length and type as on the EBSCO diskette. The differences of one character will result in download errors and garbage. The fields may be altered after downloading, however, to meet local needs.

As EBSCO also tracked out "ordered direct" titles, this downloaded invoice provided us with a database of all active subscriptions. Records were appended as new titles were added to the collection, keeping our database current. This EBSCO file formed the basis for a number of applications and other databases, both for management of the periodicals collection and for collection and for reference services.

Once the basic file was downloaded, we were able to add and alter fields as we identified opportunities to use the database. A field was added to flag titles that we receive due to our subscriptions to another title but do not track. Vendor fields enable us to identify vendors for direct titles, and to record mailing addresses for claiming. When supplemental invoices and credits began to arrive, we realized the need to add fields w record those payments and credits. The EBSCO database had four title fields of thirty characters each, which became unwieldy to index for reports. We changed the structure to two title fields of sixty characters each, using the "modify structure" and "replace" commands of dBase. This modification increased indexing speed and permitted more indexing options.

Press any key to continue...
Structure for database : C: Holdings.dbf
Number of data records : 2599
Date of last update : 07/12/89

Field	Field Name	Type	Width	Dec
1	TITLE	Character	60	
2	TITLE	Character	60	
3	ISSN	Character	9	
4	TITLENO	Numeric	9	
5	COMMENT3	Character	18	
6	HOLDINGS	Character	70	
7	HOLDINGS2	Character	70	
8	HOLDINGS3	Character	70	
9	LOCATION	Character	15	
10	MICROFORM	Character	10	
11	BIND	Character	2	
12	INACTIVE	Character	1	
13	CURR_DISPL	Character	2	
14	UPDATE	Character	1	
15	FIRST_RECD	Date	8	
16	GAP	Character	1	
Press any key to continue...				
17	FIRSTYEAR	Character	4	
18	LASTYEAR	Character	4	
19	SUBJECT1	Character	55	
20	SUBJECT2	Character	55	
21	SUBJECT3	Character	35	
22	SUBJECT4	Character	35	
" Total "			595	

Figure 9.1

Holding Section

The first project that used the new database was the production of the Currently Received Titles list. While this was a simple dBase report, it replaced an out-of-date list previously produced with a word processing package by staff in the university's data processing center.

The need for a full holdings list, which would be volume and yea specific and include inactive titles, had been recognized for some time Stetson University is over one hundred years old and has a fine collection of older journals. These inactive titles were listed on cards in special drawers of the card catalog and on the Kardex, but the information was not obvious to users. The capability was now available to use this database of current titles as the foundation for a complete list.

```
Edit : C: HOLDINGS. prg                                          Caps
| CURSOR : ◄···►        | UP DOWN              | DELETE          | Insert Mode:          Ine |
|   |Char :        Del  | | Insert line :      |        |        |                           |
| word:   Home End      | Page : PgUp  PgDn    | word:       ^T  | Save  ^W  Abort: Esc      |
| Line:   ^ ^       Find:      ^KF             | Line:        ^Y | Read file:     ^KR        |
| Reformat:^ KB         | Refind: ^KL          |                 | Write file:  ^KW          |

SET FORMAT TO HOLDINGS
SET  FUNCTION   7  TO  'MICROFILM:'                                <
SET  FUNCTION   5  TO  'MAIN COLLECTION'                           <
SET  FUNCTION   3  TO  'P.G.L.                                     <
SET  FUNCTION   8  TO  'Many volumes incomplete or missing'        <
SET  FUNCTION   6  TO  'Incomplete vols.:'                         <
SET  FUNCTION   4  TO  'Missing vols.:'                            <
SET  FUNCTION   9  TO  'MICROFICHE:'                               <
```

Figure 9.2

To create a full holdings list, the EBSCO database was copied to; Holdings database, using the quick DOS "copy" command. Additional fields were added for holdings, location, microform, and currant display space, and unnecessary fields relating to invoice information were deleted (Figure 9.1). A brief program was written to facilitate input of holding; data from the Kardex to systematize wording (Figure 9.2), and a forma for screen display and input was created (Figure 9.3). The program made it easier to use student assistants for inputting information from the Kardex. This database was then expanded by inputting records and holdings for inactive titles.

The Periodicals Holdings of Stetson University, DeLand Campus, listing 2,600 titles, was produced and distributed. It shows volume and date of holdings, any gaps, location, and formats. A copy of the holdings list, indexed by location, serves as a shelf reading list, which makes it possible to turn routine shelf-reading into a continuous inventory. An "Update" field in the database allows production of monthly cumulated supplements for title changes, additions, alteration of holdings, and deletions. A complete revision of the list is planned annually.

TITLE: AMERICAN JOURNAL OF PUBLIC HEALTH
TITLE #: 44264000

ISSN: 0090-0036 HEGIS # :01-24-20-6230 UPDATE: CURRENT DISPLAY: Y

HOLDINGS: V. 41, 1951- - v, 72, 1982 P.G.L.; V. 73, 1983 – TO DATE
BOXE INC; INCOMPLETE VOLS.(53, 57, 73) MISSING VOLS. :52
MICRO: MICORFICHE: V 77,1987 – TO DATE

SUBJECT 1 : SOCIOLOGY
SUBJECT 2: MEDICINE
SUBJECT 3:
SUBJECT 4:

LOCATION: MAIN COLLECTION BIND: M MICROFORM: MICROINHE DATE IST RECD:/

INACTIVE:

EDIT |<C:>|HOLDINGS |Rec: 115/2599 | | Cape

Figure. 9.3

Microform Database

One of the fields added to the EBSCO database, "Microform," was used to establish a microfiche control system. The command "Copy to Micro for Microform-'Microfiche' or Microform-'Microfilm' "created a separate Micro database. The structure of this database was then altered to allow tracking of both annual and quarterly shipments of microfiche and payments for them.

The dBase Assist function allowed easy creation of screen formats for rapid input of receipt and holdings data and financial information (Figure 9.4). This database also is used to create reports for the reference department with cumulative microform holdings information as each shipment is received. The microform holdings report is kept at the reference desk, and the reference librarians report it to be very helpful.

Our policy is to retain the paper copies of titles collected in microform for two years, the period of greatest use. In 1989, when the time came to dispose of the 1986 paper copies, this database was used to generate lists of titles by department, and faculty were offered the paper copies.

Title: American Journal of political Science

Title # : 2539. 01 Hegis #: 01-24-230-6270 Order Date:

Financial Records 1998 89

Period: V. 32, 1988		Total Paid:		12.44	
Invoice #: 4578321	P.O. #:P89-51	Cost:	12.20	Service:	0.24
Credit Period:					
Invoice #:	Credit #:	Credit #:.	0.00	Service:	0.00
Backorder Period:					
Invoice #:	P.O. # :	Cost:	0.00	Service:	0.00

Financial Records 1998/90

Period: V. 32, 1988		Total Paid:		12.44	
Invoice #: 4578321	P.O. #:P89-51	Cost:	12.20	Service:	0.24
Credit Period:					
Invoice #:	Credit #:	Credit #:	0.00	Service:	0.00
Backorder Period:					
Invoice #:	P.O. # :	Cost:	0.00	Service:	0.00.

Figure 9.4

Financial Database

After the first year, the advantage of using separate databases for holdings and financial information was clear. The financial data in the EBSCO database were moved to a Finance database, which then was expanded to allow the recording of financial information for five years. This allows tracking of expenditures from one year to the next, both by title and by fund charged. Fields include fund charged, cost, adjustments to cost, service charges, term covered, expiration date, and other invoice information.

The database is manually updated during the year.

The EBSCO diskette is copied to the hard disk as EBSCO.dbf, using the SDF parameter previously described to convert it to a dBase file.

Select A

Use EBSCO

Index on Titleno to Tempa

Select B

Use Finance

Index on Titleno to Tempb

Update on Titleno from A Replace Frequency with A->Frequency, New_Renew With A->New Renew, Ordernote With A->Alph Price, Start8990 With A>Startdate, Term8990 With A->Term, INV8990 With A->Invoiceno, Cost8990 With A->Cost

Although we have changed some of EBSCO's field names for our applications, these commands link the databases. It may be necessary to break this update into two segments if a great number of fields are being updated. After downloading, we return to the Finance database and use the command "SUM COST8990 FOR 'INV8890=" and compare the total with the sum generated by the same command using the EBSCO database. If there is a difference, it may be the result of an unrecorded title or title number change.

A format was created to allow viewing and editing on the screen for three years of financial data for each title.

Subject Analysis

Periodicals are assigned to academic departments and are part of those departments' library materials allocations for the year. The accounts assigned are in a field in each database (Holdings, Finance, and Micro), and reports can be easily generated for each department to show titles, expenditures, percentage increases, and microform expenditures and holdings. The perennial problem of making faculty and students aware of titles from another department which are important in their fields was solved by assigning up to four subject headings that match the curriculum to tides currently received. While it would be helpful to do the same for all tides, it was felt it would be especially useful for current tides, where browing is often a factor.

Summary

The most important advice to be offered is "Back up, back up, back up!" With your back-ups safely in hand, experiment. dBase can be exacting in requiring specificity, but it makes available an almost limitless number of informational reports as needs change. The creation of a number of specific fields for data will enable you to recall it in different combinations, some of which you may not anticipate at the time of structure design and input.

The use of dBase made possible the efficient management of our periodicals collection and fund accounting. However, with the information that can be derived from the databases, we streamlined the Kardex to include only current subscriptions. This file is scanned monthly by student assistants to identify possible claims.

We envision a full turnkey system in several years, and judicious use of dBase has made it possible to avoid the expense and trauma of an interim automated serials control system while still meeting the immediate management and reference needs of staff and users.

10

Periodical Listing and Accessioning

Introduction

There are a number of attractive features about computer-produced periodicals holdings lists which contribute to their comparative popularity. They can be produced in sufficient numbers to be distributed widely both to readers and to other libraries. They are generally much easier and more convenient to use than a card catalogue of a library's periodical holdings. New editions can be printed with very little clerical effort. Because the amount of data in a periodicals holdings list is usually very much smaller than that contained in a library's book catalogue, there are few problems involved in converting the data into machine-readable form. There are no special problems concerning the order in which periodical titles are filed, and the limited character set of a line printer is rather more acceptable here than it is when used to print a catalogue of monographs.

The idea of an automated periodicals accessioning system is very attractive because of the fairly complex clerical tasks involved in checking-in new issues, detecting and chasing parts which do not arrive on time, renewing subscriptions, and binding volumes that are complete. One of the possible outputs from an accessioning system is a list of the library's holdings, which can be printed in new editions quite frequently. In addition, lists can be printed each week showing the periodical parts which have been received during the past week.

Alternatively, such lists might record only those parts which have not been received. Either way their function is to draw readers' attention to the library's most recent periodicals. Binding records can be printed automatically when volumes are complete and can be scheduled to provide an even work load for the bindery. Subscriptions can be renewed automatically and claims made for parts that have not arrived on time.

The design of the system is geared to the regular pattern of periodical publication. This is sound design practice treating exceptions to this regular pattern as exceptions in the system. It is because such exceptions are so frequent and so varied and the procedures for handling them so comparatively complex that automated periodicals accessioning systems have not yet been so successful as they might have been.

Periodicals Published

Lists of periodicals can relate either to the holdings of one library or to the holdings of a group of libraries. In either case the list consists of a number of entries, one entry for each periodical title and for each cross reference from previous titles or alternative titles. The library's holdings of each title are given or, in the case of union lists, the holdings of each library within the group. In addition to holdings details various additional pieces of information may also be included, such as the frequency of publication, the shelf mark or other library locational symbol, and perhaps some indication of subject scope if this is not included in the shelf mark.

If the holdings list is to be produced with the needs of the library staff in mind, in addition to those of readers, then a number of additional items of information can usefully be included for each periodical. These include: the publisher, the dealer from which the library obtains the periodical, the subscription price, when it is due, the library fund it is charged to, binding information, and possibly the names of any readers to whom the journal is routed.

In fact a holdings list can come quite close to a periodicals accessioning system in the facilities it can offer. The important difference is that an accessioning system normally performs the several functions automatically in response to the data given to it, whereas a holdings list only assists human librarians in their work. Apart from the problems which have been mentioned, a decision between these two types of system might be based on the grounds of the size of a library's periodicals holdings in a way analogous to deciding where automated methods of book ordering can be justified. A large-scale operation would justify automation. However, in practice, many large libraries find that automated methods can offer no advantages over manual methods of periodicals accessioning. But a number of libraries are using computers to produce holdings lists now with the intention of extending their systems to include automated accessioning when a satisfactory method of doing this has been developed.

Each entry in a printed periodicals holdings list corresponds to one record in a machineable file. This is normally kept on magnetic tape. Each magnetic tape record has a structure corresponding to the information which is given in the printed list. Because the list must be printed in order, usually alphabetically by periodical title, provision must be made for sorting machineable records into correct order and inserting new records in the right places. A computer sort program can be used on periodical titles or, alternatively, each record can be assigned a number and the sorting can be done on this. Numbers are assigned manually so that ascending numerical sequence corresponds to correct alphabetical order of titles.

Machine File

Making: The machine file of periodicals holdings will almost invariably be created from an existing manual file. Because the manual file can be assumed to be in correct alphabetical order no machine sorting will be involved in this initial setting up of the file. A record format must be devised which will enable the computer to process the file and produce the various outputs which may be needed.

(a) Type of record.

(b) Sequence number.

(c) Title.

(d) Holdings.

(e) Shelf mark or other locational symbol.

(f) Publication frequency.

(g) Subject information.

(h) Titles or headings from which cross references are to be made, together with their reference numbers.

This information for each entry in the list is punched either into paper tape or punched cards and verified. The various categories of data in each record are identified either by specific labels or by means of a standard input format. With paper-tape input the format is specified by patterns of space and line shift characters. With input by means of punched cards the format is specified by column and card numbering. Each card in the decklet for each title is punched with the sequence number for the title, and the position of the card within the decklet is also indicated.

The program which controls the printing of the magnetic tape file makes use of this standard record format to lay each printed entry out in the desired manner. It is also possible, for example, to re-sort the file by shelf mark or subject identifier to produce a printed holdings list arranged by subject. Alternatively, a straightforward subject index to the main alphabetical sequence can be compiled.

In addition to records of a library's holdings of a particular title the printed list and the machineable magnetic tape file will also contain records for cross references and earlier forms of titles. Each of these cross-reference records must also be assigned a numerical sequence number where these are used for alphabetization purposes.

(a) Type of record.

(b) Sequence number.

(c) Title or heading referred from.

(d) Title referred to.

(e) Sequence number of title referred to.

Updating the Machine File

Entries in the holdings list for periodicals currently being received will be left "open". That is they show when a library's holdings for a title begins, but no terminal date is given. The assumption is that the library holds all volumes and parts published to date. In time, however, a number of periodicals with open entries in the holdings list will cease publication or change their titles, or the library may stop subscribing to them. The open entries will then have to be closed in order to reflect the changed nature of the library's holdings. The library will also have begun to subscribe to new journals which will require new open entries to be made in the list.

With most manual methods of producing a periodicals holdings list it is necessary to re-keyboard large sections of the entire list in order to include alterations and additions such as these to bring it up to date. But with a computer-produced list it is only necessary to keyboard the alterations and additions together with instructions as to how they axe to be added to the file. It is this ease of updating which is one major attraction of computer-produced lists of periodicals.

The procedure for updating the machine file is fairly straightforward. Where a new record is to be added to the file, a sequence number is chosen for it which will place it in the correct position in the file. (When the sequence numbers were assigned to the file in the first place, sufficient numbers were left vacant to allow for subsequent insertions into the file.)

When an existing record is to be altered it is identified by means of its sequence number. The type of alteration is specified: whether it is to be a deletion, addition, or replacement, and the section of the original record to be altered is indicated.

Printing the List

The updated machine file can be printed either by line printer, or by tape typewriter using a paper-tape intermediary. Where the list is a long one it will probably be more convenient to use a line printer, and although the quality of printing it can produce is rather inferior to that of a typewriter, good layout can go far towards increasing legibility.

The output from typewriter or line printer is cut into page or column-size lengths. These are reduced photographically and printed by offset-litho methods.

Automated Periodicals Accessioning

The kind of list that has been discussed so far can indicate a library's periodicals holdings by means of closed entries for inactive titles and open entries for titles that are currently being received. It can be brought up to date comparatively easily by human decisions about the additions and changes that need to be made to it. The instructions and data required for these changes must be converted to machine-readable form and input to a computer run, which updates the magnetic-tape version of the holdings list and prints it.

Automated Periodicals Methods

In the system which has so far achieved the greatest popularity, the computer punches a deck of eighty-column cards as a result of this forecasting operation; one card for each periodical part, supplement, title page, index, etc., that is expected to arrive in the library during the period of the forecast. In most medium-sized libraries one month is a convenient period. A smaller library might opt for a longer period, while a larger library would probably want to reduce the period to a fortnight in order to keep the file within manageable proportions. Each card in the file is punched and interpreted with data sufficient to enable the corresponding periodical part to be identified and processed.

The work of the periodicals checking-in clerk under such an automated system is as follows. For each periodical issue that is received in the library the corresponding punched card is pulled from the card file. It will contain all necessary instructions for the clerk; the shelf mark to be written on the periodical, the library branch or department where it is to be sent, and possibly any routing instructions that may apply to it. The periodical is sent for despatch to the appropriate destination and its punched card placed into a special "received" file.

Cards in this file representing periodical issues now received in the library can serve a number of purposes. They can be printed to give a daily listing of new periodicals arrived in the library. Cumulated weekly or fortnightly listings can be made or, alternatively, such lists can include only those periodicals which were expected to arrive but have not arrived. Because a periodical's full title is not normally included in the card in order to save space, a computer run is required if these lists are to contain full titles. Finally, each month, cards in this "received" file are used to update the main periodicals holdings file. At this run the next month's batch of cards is punched.

Cards still remaining in the file represent parts that are overdue. Claims can be made for these after they have been considered by the librarian in charge of periodicals.

The monthly processing run also reports on volumes that have been completed and are now ready for binding.

Detailed Method

It is convenient for records to be of fixed length, with overspill records for those few titles which have an unusually large amount of information associated with them. As in the case of the machineable file for a system producing a straightforward periodic listing of holdings, edch record in this file is assigned a reference number. This provides the facility for simple unique identification of each record in the file and may also act as a sorting key for arranging periodical titles in alphabetical order. The data contained in each record in this file must be equivalent to that contained in conventional manual card files, but in addition it must enable the computer to calculate when to expect new issues.

The following information is therefore likely to be required for each record in the file:

1. Record identification number.
2. Coden or other short mnemonic identification tag.
3. Title.
4. Sub-title.
5. Previous titles from which cross references have been made, together with the record identification number of each reference.
6. Shelf mark or class mark.
7. Subject descriptors.
8. Number of copies.
9. Their library locations and routing.
10. Complete holdings information including bound and unbound volumes and volumes held as microforms.
11. Frequency of publication.
12. Sample average date of arrival.
13. Number of issues per volume.
14. Bookseller or supplier.

15. Library fund charged to and subscription number (if any).
16. Annual subscription,
17. Date when subscription is due for renewal.
18. Reordering procedure.
19. Binding instructions including treatment of title page, table of contents, index, advertisements, covers, etc.

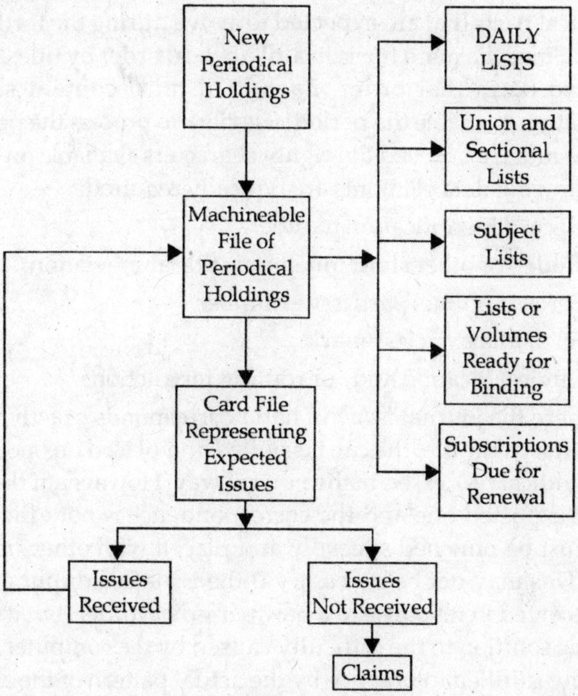

Figure 10.1. Automatic periodicals accessioning system

Each record can contain a relatively large amount of information, so it is necessary to encode certain categories of data to keep the record within a reasonable size. This can be done conveniently for such items as the bookseller, library fund, reordering procedure, and other additional information where there are only a limited number of different possibilities.

When the system is being set up in the first instance and whenever new records are being added to the magnetic tape file, a fairly complex clerical process is involved in translating the data on the original old manual record cards into the form in which it must appear in the machine record. In many cases considerable experience of periodicals librarianship is required for this, so that it becomes realistic to create a temporary record to facilitate the conversion process. A librarian creates a written record in exactly the same format as the machine record, and a clerk keypunches directly from this.

Each month a computer run punches a deck of cards for the periodical parts that are expected to arrive during the forthcoming month. Since the main file is in alphabetical order by title, the cards will also be in that order. Each card must contain sufficient information to enable the periodicals clerk to process the periodical, and this must not exceed the eighty characters available on the card. The following data elements are typically required:

- Record identification number.
- Coden or other short mnemonic title abbreviation.
- Series, volume, part, issue number.
- Shelf mark or class mark.
- Library location and/or routing instructions.

Where the journal issue in hand corresponds exactly with the card that is in the file, the card is pulled and placed on one side and the periodical processed in the normal way. However, if the issue is not the expected one and the correspondence is not exact, then a card must be punched specially and placed with other "received" cards. This may not be necessary if the issue is a duplicate or has been received in response to a new periodical order, but it remains the basic solution to the difficulty caused by the computer forecast not being fulfilled in practice by the actual pattern of the arrival in the library of periodical parts. It is a slow procedure to punch an eighty-column card and verify it, compared with the relatively quick job of pulling one card from a file. The extent to which the computer forecast is accurate, that is the extent to which the future publication pattern of a periodical is the same as or can be predicted from the present publication pattern, is a measure of the probable success of a periodicals accessioning of this type.

However, as with other automated library systems, once the data has been put into the system and included in the machineable holdings record, then a number of different outputs can be produced without any further manual intervention. These may well provide the justification for an automated system where they can be shown to be useful.

If the library needs a frequent listing of newly received periodical parts for public consultation, then this can be produced easily by the computer. A computer run is required for this if the eighty-column cards for expected issues do not contain the title in a form readily understood by library users. Such frequent listings can be especially valuable in a library system with a number of branches, in each of which current periodicals are displayed. A listing can then be made for each branch and copies displayed in other branches, or one union list can be made.

One copy of a fully detailed printed holdings list can be kept conveniently at each public service point to facilitate the answering of readers' queries. This is especially valuable in a library with a number of branches, for a card catalogue of the periodical holdings of the library system is not likely to be available at each branch. If a subject index can be prepared for this detailed holdings list, or if it can also be printed in subject order, then its value will be considerably enhanced.

The facility for automatic notification of volumes that are ready for binding has already been mentioned. This can be especially valuable in a large library and eliminates manual checking of shelves to see which volumes are ready for binding. It requires a high degree of systematization of binding procedures and cannot, of course, make allowances for volumes from which parts have been borrowed or lost.

One important advantage the system has to offer is that it shows up those periodical issues which have not arrived at the end of each month. Their punched cards will be left in the file of expected arrivals. The periodicals librarian must decide for each of them whether to initiate a claims procedure or to file the card into the new month's file. Cards in each month's arrival file can be colour coded so that it is possible to recognize cards representing issues more than one month overdue. The actual claims notice can either be printed by the computer or prepared manually.

System Designs

The above automated periodicals accessioning system is unsatisfactory in two major respects. The clerical routines required for checking-in periodicals are scarcely any faster than those of conventional manual systems. Both require the periodical to be processed by hand and both include a file look-up. It is more difficult to read the interpreted punched cards of the computer system than the typed headings on manual cards, but quicker to pull a card and place it in the "received" bin than write brief information about the issue in hand onto a manual card. Exceptions to the regular pattern demand a fair amount of key-punching effort.

Access to the file of expected arrivals is speeded up if, instead of a deck of cards, a printout is made containing roughly the same information for each part that is punched into the cards. It is possible, however, to print the full title of each periodical because the restriction to eighty characters no longer applies. Parts are simply ticked off on a list as they arrive. At the end of the month only briefest details of parts that have not arrived need be punched, for example the serial number of the part in that monthly printout. But the whole list must be searched to find those parts that have been delayed. When unexpected issues arrive in the library, these can be entered manually on the list and keypunched at the end of the month in a highly abbreviated coded form. One possible disadvantage with this type of system is that frequent lists of recently arrived parts cannot be prepared. All other outputs are possible, however, and it is not necessary to use the computer at any time other than when a printout of expected issues is made.

Another alternative provides greater flexibility at the expense of more manual keyboarding. A card, edge-punched with paper-tape code, is punched for each periodical title in the collection. Punched into each card are the title and record identification number of the periodical and written on it is all the information required to process each periodical issue. The procedure for checking-in each issue is as follows.

The edge-punched card for the title is pulled from the file. It is then run through the reading head of a tape typewriter which causes the data punched into the title card to be punched into a paper tape. Details of the volume and part number of the issue in hand are then punched manually into the paper tape and the title card is returned to the file. The paper tape thus contains machine-readable information about all periodical parts that have been received. It is exactly analogous to the file of punched cards which represent

.received parts in the standard punched-card system and can be used to provide the same range of outputs. One disadvantage of the tape system is that periodical parts which do not arrive on time are not represented by cards remaining in the file: the computer must make a special listing of them instead. Considerably more staff time is required for routine checking-in than with the punched-card system. Since manual keyboarding is the regular procedure, irregularities in the arrival pattern of periodicals do not cause the same disturbance as in the punched-card system.

This is a dual problem facing any system for accessioning periodicals automatically and a solution that is entirely satisfactory does not yet appear to have emerged. The checking-in procedure must be quick if it is to match the great efficiency in this respect of manual accessioning systems. Thus almost all manual keyboarding is ruled out except where it is of very limited extent, and it should preferably be needed only for exceptions to the general rule. Secondly, the system design must be flexible enough to cater easily for the many irregularities which are superimposed on the underlying regular pattern of periodical publication.

11

Periodical Selection through Computers

The collection of active periodicals is one of the library's most highly used facets, providing as it does access to current thinking in the human services. However, the library also owns a large number of "dead runs" of older periodicals (i.e., publications that have ceased to publish), which are retained for archival and historical purposes. We, of course, have our share of shelf-space woes (perhaps more than our share), and consequently all of our dead runs and even a portion of our live runs are shelved outside the library proper, in various closets and classrooms throughout the School of Social Work. Over the years, this has made the procedure of retrieving periodical issues from the collection ever more complicated, as the number of possible periodical locations has grown.

Obviously, what we needed was a periodicals location/ holdings list, both for our own purposes and to serve the needs of our users. A dBase III database seemed to offer great flexibility and ease of updating, and had the additional feature of allowing limited subject indexing, which was something we had often contemplated producing for our periodical collection.

The library's computer is an IBM-compatible Compaq Portable Personal Computer, with 256 kilobytes of memory and two disk drives. Recently upgraded our memory to 640 kilobytes, which has improved the efficiency of some of the procedures described here. However, only 256 kilobytes of memory was required to support the project described.

Need to Data base

The first phase of the project was the creation of the structure of the database. Kristen, who was then the technical services intern librarian, analyzed the periodical access needs of the library, and designed the field structure as shown in Fig. 11.1.

Six fields may not seem like a great deal of information, but it was sufficient for our needs. (Note that this database is maintained solely for the purpose of providing access lists - check-in, claiming, binding, and other procedures are recorded elsewhere.) It is a fairly simple task to add additional fields as unforeseen needs arise.

The CONT field is a continuation field for additional title information, such as former or subsequent title or issuing body. The LOCATION field contains a two-character location code. HOLDINGS shows the dates owned by the library.

With the database structure in place, the entry of individual records was begun. Most periodical information was taken directly from the periodical check-in file, but because some of the older records (especially those for dead runs) were doubtful, examination of the actual volumes was necessary in many cases. Ultimately, a complete inventory was made of periodicals outside the library proper, and this information was entered into the database.

Field Name	Data Type	Field Length
TITLE	Character	65
CONT	Character	100
LOCATION	Character	2
HOLDINGS	Character	20
SUBJECT1	Character	35
SUBJECT2	Character	35

Figure 11.1

Subject analysis was undertaken by Kristen and Ann Collins, another intern librarian. Issues of each periodical were examined, taking special note of statements of purpose. Most of the headings were adapted from those used by Psychological Abstracts and the Library of Congress. A few form headings, such as NEWSPAPERS and POPULAR MAGAZINES, were used.

Once the record for each periodical title had been entered, it was easy to produce alphabetical title/location/holdings lists using the Create Report command. We could print as few or as many of the database fields as we wanted (as long as there was space on the page). Printing out a list arranged by subject heading turned out to be quite difficult indeed. In fact, at first it seemed impossible. In order to print out a list in which each periodical title will be listed twice - once under each of two different subject headings - it is necessary to combine the two subject heading fields temporarily into one field. dBase III offers no straightforward or obvious method for doing this.

Kristen was on the verge of abandoning the second subject heading for each periodical title when Ann recommended she read an article by Jim Gillespie ("Using dBase to Create Book Catalogs with Two Subject Headings," Small Computers in Libraries) which delineated an ingenious method of merging subject fields using the Modify Structure command. Briefly, the method entails making two new databases from the original periodicals database (one containing SUBJECT 1, the other SUBJECT 2) and renaming one of the subject fields so that they each have the same name. The subject fields can then be combined using the Append command, and a subject heading list can be printed. Using this method, we soon had our first periodical subject heading list.

Maintenance of Database

Changes to the periodicals database - in the form of additions, deletions, name changes, and corrections - occur in an unpredictable manner. Some months bring many changes; others bring none. I wanted an updating procedure that would be flexible enough to allow me to print new lists as needed - semi-annually, bi-monthly, monthly, or even weekly – with a minimum of difficulty.

The two methods available to me were not wholly satisfactory. One method was to use the dBase III+ Assistant Menu. The Assistant seems to have been designed to offer a large number of options that may be understood without reference to supporting documentation.

Consequently, the system is fairly flexible, but the large number of options and the somewhat awkward menu structure make for slow updating. The other method involved referring to a locally produced manual listing the commands needed for each updating procedure. These commands were issued from the dot prompt, and while this method was quicker than using the Assistant.

Main Menu — SSW Periodical Database

A ADD new records

E EDIT existing records

D DELETE records

M MERGE subject fields (must be done before printing subject list)

P PRINT lists

Q QUIT

Enter letter of your choice:

Figure 11.2

Enter or edit a periodicals record

Enter a carriage return in last field to exit/save.

PERIODICAL TITLE: ________________

(Capitalize 1 st Letters)

OTHER TITLE INFORMATION: ________________

('Continued by' or 'Continues' notes)

LOCATION: ________________

(PR, PE, BR, FF, OR, OF)

HOLDINGS: ________________

SUBJECT HEADING 1: ________________

(use CAPITALS)

SUBJECT HEADING 2: ________________

(use CAPITALS; enter ZZZ if blank)

Figure 11.3

Main Menu

1. Adding new records
2. Editing existing records

3. Deleting unwanted records
4. Merging subject fields
5. Printing lists

This list was converted into the Main Menu screen with very little revision (Fig. 11.2). Selecting one of the Main Menu options displays a submenu, a further prompt, or a database record, depending on the complexity of the task involved.

SEARCH SUBMENU (For editing and deleting)

T Search for record by periodical TITLE
N Search for record by record NUMBER
F Move FORWARD to next record
B Move BACK to previous record
R RETURN to Main Menu Enter letter of your choice:

Figure 11.4

DELETE SUBMENU

N NORMAL delete (using title or record number)
F FAST delete (record number only)
R RETURN to Main Menu

Enter letter of your choice:

Figure 11.5

Adding Records

The ADD option displays a blank record, ready for user input. The display was achieved through the use of a format file, which allowed me to customize the input screen to suit the database including brief instructions for the user (Figure 11.3). When the record has been entered, the user may add additional records to the database, or may return to the Main Menu.

Updating Records

The EDIT option displays the Search Submenu (Figure 11.4). The first two search options allow the user to specify the title or record number of the desired record. The system then searches for the record and, if found, displays the record for editing. The second two options move the pointer to the next or previous record (one record number higher or lower). These options serve as rather clumsy substitutes for the Page Up and Page Down keys that the Assistant uses while in the Edit mode.

Deleting Records

The DELETE option displays the Delete Submenu (Figure 11.5). The NORMAL delete option displays the Search Submenu - the same Submenu used for editing - which allows the user to search for the record to be deleted. The FAST delete option provides a much quicker search procedure when the record number is already known. The user is asked to enter a record number, and the record is deleted immediately. This is especially useful when a group of records needs deleting, as they can be located and deleted in rapid succession.

Merging

The MERGE procedure did not lend itself easily to dBase III+ programming. At first I attempted to translate the Gillespie method directly into program statements. This worked, but only with substantial participation from the user, which seemed to me to defeat the purpose of the main menu system. I then tried several modifications of the Gillespie method, including the use of the Structure Extended command, which allows database structure to be modified during the execution of a program. This last method seemed very promising, but I ran into a snag when I found that a field whose name is changed becomes a blank field, and therefore useless.

1. From the main database, make two smaller databases: One containing the fields TITLE and SUBJECT1 (call it SPLIT1), the other containing the fields TITLE and SUBIECT 2.
2. Make a copy of SPLITI (call it SPARE) and set SPLIT1 aside.
3. One by one, access each record of both SPARE and SPLITI and do the following:

A. Use SPLIT2. Copy SUBJECT2 into a memory variable.

B. Use SPARE. Replace SUBJECT1 with the contents of the memory variable.

When this bucket brigade process is completed, the field named SUBJECT1 in SPARE will actually contain SUBJECT2 field contents. SPARE will be identical to SPLIT2 except for the difference in field names.

4. Combine SPLITI (TITLE and SUBJEC`I'1 fields) with SPARE (TITLE ar d SUBJECT1 - now actually SUBJECT 2 - fields).

PRINT SUBMENU

A Print SSW Periodicals List (Title, location & holdings fields)
B Print Subject Index (A title list, arranged by subject)
C Print Full Periodicals List (All fields; for office use only)
R Return to main menu

Enter letter of your choice:

Figure 11.6

CHILD AND YOUTH CARE QUARTERLY
Continues Child Care Quarterly

LOCATION: PR	ISSN: 0893-0848
DATES HELD: 1987-	MICRO DATES: 1987
VOLS. HELD: v.16-	MICRO VOLS.: v.16

SUBJECT 1: DAY CARE
SUBJECT 2: CHILDREN AND ADOLESCENTS

Figure 11.7

Hardcopy of List

The PRINT option displays the Print Submenu (Figure 11.6). The "A" choice (SSW Periodicals List) prints the list we make available to the public. It contains only the TITLE, LOCATION and HOLDINGS fields, and is designed to serve as a, quick reference to our periodical collection. The "B" choice (Subject Index) prints a list of our periodical titles arranged by subject. The "C" choice (Full Periodicals List) prints all the fields for each record in the database. This list is used by the technical services intern as a quick reference and as a working copy for noting changes.

All three lists were formatted by writing special printing procedures. These procedures can be as simple or as complicated as the programmer wishes, but the basic objective is to tell the computer which fields to print and where to print them. Figure 11.7 shows a sample record, formatted as it appears in our Full Periodicals List (for office use). Note that I have added a few new fields to the database; MICRO stands for microfilm.

It should be plain to anyone with a little programming experience that one could tinker endlessly with a set of procedures such as these. (A time display could be added to menus; more search options could be added; help screens could be provided. At present, I am modifying the delete procedures to allow more Pack and Recall options.)

12

Indexing with Computers

Introduction & Uses

There has been a great deal of interest recently in text-based applies Lions of popular database management software programs such a dBase III+. Ashon-Tate's dBase III+ is widely regarded as one of the most versatile, powerful, and useful database management program for IBM and IBM-compatible microcomputers. Moreover, the program has been touted in the literature as an excellent choice for librarians wishing to automate a wide range of library functions.

Because of such articles, and plenty of slick advertising copy dBase III+ may now be found in libraries of all sizes, specialties, and levels. Unfortunately, what the advertising copy does not make clear is that the real price of the power and versatility of dBase III+ becomes apparent later when attempting to manipulate data with the program. A major drawback of dBase III+, as anyone who has at tempted to accomplish even moderately difficult tasks with the program knows, is that in order to derive full benefit from the program one must achieve a working knowledge of the dBase III+ program mine language. Despite this drawback, which is not insignificant dBase III+ should continue to be explored as a tool for generating needed reference sources, such as in-house databases and indexes to these local files.

Reference librarians will readily agree that newspapers are a good source of information, particularly for research topics involving current affairs or local history. It is also true, however, that effective use of these library resources is usually hampered by inadequate or completely absent indexing.

At the Chicano Resource Center (CRC) at California State University-Fullerton, we have successfully used dBase III+ and a word processor (WordStar) to generate a printed subject index to articles about Chicanos in a number of newspapers currently received by the university library. As a finding tool, the printed index has been extremely useful for undergraduate and graduate students working on Hispanic-related research projects. The use of dBase III+ towards this end enables the small and constantly changing number of student assistants who make up the staff of the CRC to maintain an up-to-date citation database and to generate attractive, well-formatted, and useful indexes.

In addition to the monthly index, the CRC maintains a well organized clippings file, Since most of the articles from the various newspapers are cut out and filed, in essence, the full-text of the articles indexed is made available to library researchers. The combination of the index and the full-text of the articles makes this a truly useful resource provided by the CRC.

To encourage continued experimentation with dBase III+ in libraries, we will describe here the short dBase III+ procedure files that we have developed. Working with previously created bibliographic databases, these programs are used to produce a subject listing of newspaper citations to a disk file. This file is then displayed on the screen or else printed on paper. Librarians and others hoping to provide access to such publications as local and campus newspapers, and who have access to dBase III+, are encouraged to request and try the programs to generate such indexes. All the dBase III+ programs and database files necessary to create such an index are described here. The following discussion of the program functions and dBase III+ commands assume a working knowledge of the dBase III+ program, but makes no such assumptions regarding familiarity or experience with the dBase III+ programming language.

The program listings (source code) may be created using either the dBase III+ word processor or another word processor of choice, as long as it may generate ASCII files.

Hardware & Software Requirements

- a system hardware configuration which includes a hard disk drive and at least 512 kilobytes of internal system memory
- a basic familiarity with dBase III+ commands
- a word processor (other than dBase III+ 's) to achieve final formatting of the subject index file
- a line printer attached to the microcomputer for printing of the index

Pre-requirement for Software

The following steps must be completed before running the master menu program:

- The four dBase III+ programs described below must be created using the dBase III+ word processor (using the "Modify Command" instruction from within dBase III+) or by using another word processing program.
- The three database files identified below must be created using the dBase III+ "Create" command.

Assuming that the minimum requirements listed above are met, dBase III+ should be used to create a citation database file, a subject heading database file, and a temporary holding file. In order for the program to work properly, these files must be named "DATABASE. DBF," "DATERMS. DBF," and "HEAD. DBF" respectively. Figures 12.1 through 3 represent the respective database structures.

Database Working with .DBF

This database file may be thought of as the master database file which contains all the elements of the bibliographic citation and the numeric codes for subject headings assigned. The database structure shown in Figure 12.1 indicates the names of the various fields in each record.

AUTHOR (Optional)

The optional AUTHOR field is to be used for the names(s) of the author(s). This field is optional because the supplied version of the subject program will not print the contents of the AUTHOR field as part of the subject index. The existence or nonexistence of the

AUTHOR field will not affect the execution of the subject program. It is recommended that the field be used, however, in case an author (byline) listing may be required anytime in the future.

Structure for database: c: Database.dbf
Number of data records: 0
Date of last update: 07/17/87

Field	Field Name	Type	Width	Dec
1	AUTHOR	Character	40	
2	TITLE	Character	70	
3	DATE	Date	8	
4	PAGE	Character	7	
5	HEAD1	Character	4	
6	HEAD2	Character	4	
7	HEAD3	Character	4	
8	HEAD4	Character	4	
9	HEAD5	Character	4	
10	HEAD6	Character	4	
11	HEAD7	Character	4	
12	HEADB	Character	4	
13	HEAD9	Character	4	
14	HEAD10	Character	4	
** Total **			166	

Figure 12.1

TITLE

The TITLE field allows for the entry of the first seventy characters of the title or headline. In practice, this length has proved to be adequate given the newspaper's tendency to save space by truncating, abbreviating, and otherwise shortening descriptive titles. As a practical sorting consideration, when entering headlines, initial articles such as "a," "an," and "the" in the title field are transposed to the end.

DATE

This field will contain the date of the newspaper article. Please note that this field is designated as a "date" field as provided for in dBase III+ and that the date will be entered in the form of month, day, and year (MM/DD/YY).

PAGE

The PAGE field allows for seven characters to accommodate those newspapers, such as the Los Angeles Times, that use alphanumeric page numbers.

HEAD (1-10)

The HEAD fields (1-10) will contain the code numbers for the subject headings assigned to that particular citation. The fact that there can be as many as ten different headings assigned to any one citation is the major contribution of this program. If needed, this limitation could easily be modified upward or downward as deemed appropriate. Typically, our newspaper articles are assigned an average of four subject headings to describe the content. Because the very same subject headings are assigned repeatedly to different citations, it is much more efficient use of disk space to encode them into smaller units and thereby save critical disk space.

Structure for database: c:Dataterms.dbf
Number of data records: 0
Date of last update: 07/17/87

Field	Field Name	Type	Width	Dec
1	NO	Character	4	
2	TERM	Character	60	
	** Total **		65	

Figure 12.2

Database Working with .DBF

The second database file, DATERMS.DBF (Figure 12.2), will contain the text of the subject headings selected for use with citations and their corresponding code numbers. The code numbers arc those which will ultimately be entered in the HEAD (1-10) fields of DATABASE.DBF. This particular database may be thought of as the authority file for your indexing vocabulary.

CODENO

This field contains the unique four-digit code number for the subject heading used to describe the newspaper article. The subject is encoded so that a subject heading of up to sixty characters may be represented by no more than four characters. Since the same subject terms are reused constantly, the practice of encoding the headings results in significant savings of precious disk space.

Structure for database: c:head.dbf
Number of data records: 0
Date of last update: 07/13/87

Field	Field Name	Type	Width	Dec
1	CITNO	Character	4	
2	HEAD1	Character	4	
** Total **				9

Figure 12.3. Structure for Temporary File

TERM

This field contains the text of the subject headings selected for use. Once the term has been established along with its corresponding number in the CODENO field, the term may be used as needed by simply entering the CODENO code number in the DATABASE.DBF fields HEAD (1-10).

HEAD.DBF

This database file is a temporary working file that the main program uses to store the relationship between the citation numbers in the DATABASE.DBF and the codes for the index temps in the TERMS.DBF file (Figure 12.3). The use of this file is completely transparent to the user. The program will use the file without any knowledge or intervention on the part of the user; nevertheless, the file must exist on the same subdirectory and must be available for the use of the program. The user is required to create the database file (using the dBase III+ "CREATE" command) prior to running the program, but it is not required to enter any data in any of its fields.

The Programs of Database

The Master Menu-Drawing Program

This program controls the overall execution of the program. It is used to draw the screen which contains the master menu of options.

Options are selected from the menu and executed in strict order to ensure correct operation of the program modules.

The Data-Linking Program (DATAHEAD.PRG)

The first dBase III+ program called from the menu program is the DATAHEAD.PRG program. This program first sorts the data by date and then extracts subject heading information from the resulting DATABASE.DBF file and copies it to a text file named TRMNO.TXT. This text file will be needed temporarily to establish the link with the subject heading codes in the DATERMS.DBF file.

The DATAHEAD2 Program

This program is used to create a small database consisting of the data in the TRMNO.TXT file. The program opens the database file HEAD.DBF and appends the data from the TRMNO.TXT file. This data is then manipulated for later use by the subject program.

The Subject Index Generating Program: This program is the workhorse of the group. The program sets aside three separate working areas, opens and places the three files in their respective work areas, and extracts the information as needed to generate the completed subject index. In addition, this program formats the output along pre-established formats. Finally, this program creates a text file named SUBJ_NDX.TXT to hold the finished index. It is this file that is read into our WordStar program for finishing touches, such as running heads, pagination, etc.

Uses of Programme

In order to generate a printed index, the following procedure is followed.

1. Using dBase III+ 's APPEND command, we enter the bibliographic data in the DATABASE.DBF. The HEAD (1.10) fields are temporarily left blank.
2. Using dBase III+ 's CREATE REPORT command, a triplespaced printout of the citation is generated. This "edit list" is used as a worksheet to assign subject headings to individual citations.
3. The text of the subject terms pencilled in the edit list is used to create records in the DATERMS.DBF file. Once again APPEND is used to create the records in the DA TERMS.DBF. The first field, CODENO is assigned a unique four-digit number that

will represent the term henceforth Numbers in the CODENO field are assigned sequentially be ginning with 0001.

4. The encoded subject headings are entered into the database file. This is accomplished by entering the numbers representing subject headings, which are found in the CODENO field of the DATERMS.DBF field, in the HEAD (1-10) fields in the DATABASE.DBF file. Care is taken to fill in leading blanks with "0"s for numbers that have less than four digits (numbers less than 1,000).
5. The data entered in both database files should be checked for completeness and accuracy. Once satisfied with the integrity of the data, the subject program may be run.

```
NEWSPAPER INDEXING PROGRAM

1.  LINK DATABASE FILES
2.  CREATE LOOKUP FILES
3. CREATE SUBJECT INDEX

0.  Exit
                Select  0
```

Figure 12.4

The program DATAMAST.PRG displays a menu with three options (Figure 12.4). These options should all be selected in sequence. The DATAMAST.PRG program takes the two user database files, DATABASE.DBF and DATERMS.DBF and, in turn, sorts, indexes, and otherwise prepares them for use to generate the subject index. The finished subject output is directed to a disk file named SUBJ NDX.TXT which may then be edited by a word processing program, such as Wordstar, to generate a final, formatted subject index printout.

13

Ordering and Acquisition

Overview

In general terms a computer-aided ordering system performs the following functions. It prepares orders to be sent to booksellers and keeps a record of all current outstanding orders. Where there is any undue delay on the part of the bookseller in supplying a book, the system prepares a reminder note or "chaser". When books are received in the library, the computer handles the various associated accounting procedures and enables the state of the library's book funds to be reported frequently to the librarian. It produces an accessions register as a by-product of the system, and may also provide processing slips which accompany the books as they go to the cataloguing department. In some cases the bibliographic data comprising the order record is simply amended by cataloguing staff in order to produce a catalogue record. This can make for economies in the cataloguing process and may facilitate the compilation of a shelf list in machine-readable form. Where a library uses a computerized circulation system which embodies mechanical collection of charging data, the necessary machine-readable book cards may readily be punched automatically as part of the acquisition process. A wide variety of statistical analyses and compilations can readily be derived from the ordering process. These can take many forms; they may concentrate on the types of books the library purchases and what they cost; or, alternatively, may be directed to the booksellers and the quality of service they give. This can often be very valuable to a library seeking to make its ordering procedure as efficient as possible. An automated ordering system facilitates various kinds of reporting. Statistics are one kind, others include lists of books on order and in process for use of library staff and readers, and, in university libraries, reports to departments on the progress of the book orders originating from them.

Automated Ordering System

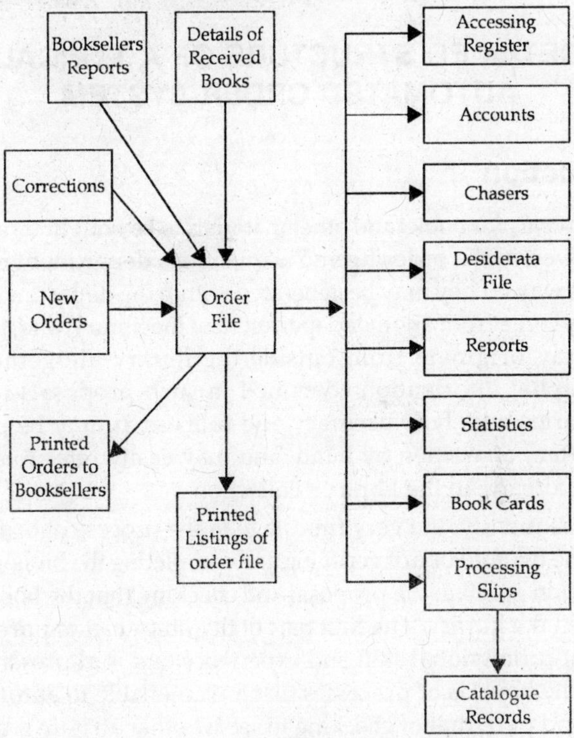

Figure 13.1. Automated order system

The overall structure of a typical automated order system is represented diagrammatically. It is seen that the central part of the system is a file of records of books on order and in process. This is kept on magnetic tape but may sometimes be transferred to magnetic disc during processing. New records are added to the file as books are ordered, existing order records are added to and modified as books arrive or as booksellers report on their availability. Among the various outputs which are derived from the machineable order file are chasers to booksellers, reports to originating departments, statistical analyses, and accounting information. The order file can be printed after having been sorted into the required order. Typical arrangements of the printed file are; by date of order, by order number, and by author and title. When books have been processed and have taken their places on the library shelves, the order records maybe used to produce processing slips, book cards, catalogue records, and an accessions register.

DETAILED STRUCTURE OF A TYPICAL AUTOMATED ORDER SYSTEM

Introduction

Proposals for books and other materials to be bought by a library are received in the ordering and acquisitions department in many different ways. They may be generated within the department itself, they may come from another department of the library, and, in many cases, may originate from outside the library altogether. The bibliographic information contained in such proposals for new books varies widely in accuracy and fullness. It may be printed, typewritten, or written by hand, and may easily refer to an item which is already in the library's collection.

Consequently, the very first stage in the process of ordering a book is the twofold one of verifying and completing the bibliographic information given in the proposal and checking that the book is not already in the library. The first part of this stage can require a high degree of professional skill and experience and is at present quite outside the bounds of processes that are amenable to automation. The second part, that of checking to see whether an item is already in the library, is essentially a catalogue look-up process and is, in principle, capable of automation. The fact that it is a tiresome clerical chore makes its automation more desirable. It could be accomplished by a computer in a straightforward matching operation – matching the proposal record against catalogue records-if the library's catalogue were in machine-readable form and if it were certain that the catalogue record would be exactly the same as the proposal record. Even if the matching process were only carried so as to include author's name, full title, and edition, this is making verv great demands on the accuracy, fullness, and consistency of library catalogue. No librarian can always be certain of being able to cite an author's name consistently, fully, and accurately, never to omit part of a title from a catalogue record, or to be consistent in edition statements. The computer program which controls the matching process can be written so as to allow for a certain inconsistency in the construction of the catalogue records and thus widen the scope of the matching. This increases the chance of erroneous matchings and demands that the results of the computer match be edited by hand. Because of these difficulties, this part of the ordering process has not yet been automated.

Scope of Automated Ordering System

In order to bring the proposal record within the scope of the automated order system it must first be converted into machineable form. To do this, any one of the standard methods for preparing data for input to a computer system may be used; punched cards, paper tape, or even magnetic tape or on-line data input directly to the computer. At this stage it becomes necessary to specify the various sections of the order record so that the computer can recognize them and process them correctly. One cannot assume that the computer is itself able to distinguish the author of a book from its date of publication, or the name of the publisher from a library classification number. Not only must the sections of the order record be identified or labelled, but the format of the record must be designed so as to allow for all eventualities. Enough data must be included to enable all the desired outputs from the machine to be produced, and the format must be hospitable enough to cater for all the varied items which the system must process.

There are two principal ways in which the several parts of the order record can be identified for the computer. Either the format of the record as it is typed on a tape typewriter or punched onto cards is designed so as to be machine-interpretable, or the sections of the record are labelled explicitly.

The structure of the order record is not dissimilar to that of a catalogue record, but it should be emphasized that there are certain important differences. In the order record it is usually quite satisfactory to treat the author and descriptive statement together as one unit, whereas this is not possible in a catalogue record. On the other hand, other items of information, comparatively unimportant in a catalogue record, become important in the ordering process. Good examples of this are the price of the book, the bookseller, and the book fund from which it is to be purchased.

Some automated ordering systems are so designed that the legible hard copy, produced when order records are converted to machine-readable form, is used as the actual orders which are sent to the booksellers. Other systems print the orders on the computer line printer and use the hard copy of the keypunching operation just to check the accuracy of the ordering data. In other instances the odd mistake is regarded as being of little importance and the hard copy is discarded or, alternatively, the keypuncher can work "blind", having no visible record at all of what has been typed.

There are advantages in both of these two alternative ways of producing the printed orders which are sent to booksellers. Where the keypunching hard copy is sent to the booksellers, the order department must, group together batches of orders which are to be sent to one bookseller and keypunch them as a group. This manual sorting operation is transferred to the computer if orders are printed on the line printer. However, where orders are not printed by the computer the library is free from the need to make a computer run before a new batch of orders can be sent off. Thus, new orders can easily be sent off daily, whereas it could be difficult to justify a daily computer run for this purpose, except in the largest libraries. Where a library purchases many second-hand books, where speed in ordering is vital, this factor becomes very important. It is, of course, possible to have a combination of the two systems, in which the keypunching hard copy is used for rush orders.

Additional Information

If orders are to be sent to the booksellers as output from the line printer then it is convenient to keep a magnetic tape file of the names and addresses of the booksellers with whom the library deals. Each bookseller is given a simple code number and this is used when keypunching the original order records in order to save time. Procedures must exist for adding new booksellers to the file and removing old ones from it. Because some books will be bought from unusual sources never likely to be used again, an alternative routine must be provided whereby the full address of the source can be given in the order record without including it in the bookseller's file.

When a book arrives in the library in response to an order the system must be told about this, and this demands a further category of input data. The actual price that is being charged for the book can be included along with this data. It may be different from the price given in the original order record. At this stage it may also be necessary to amend any part of the bibliographic information in the order record, although this can alternatively be postponed until after the book has been catalogued.

In order to produce entries for an accessions register it may be necessary to supply the computer with the accession number that has been assigned to each book. This can be included along with the information that the book has been received in the library. Alternatively the machine itself can assign accession numbers and report them to the library staff when it prints processing slips. There are innumerable possibilities to suit the many various ways of doing the same job.

Finally, it will be necessary to make corrections and alterations to existing records in the order file. The computer can readily check for some errors in all of the above types of input data and report back on each faulty record and the type of mistake in it. The mistake is then corrected at the next computer run. Sometimes, alterations are required, to bookseller's reports, for example, when items are delayed longer than was originally expected.

Result of System

The main machineable file of records of books on order is kept arranged by order number. The week's new orders are added to the end of the order file where they will be in correct sequence since the new order numbers assigned to them run on consecutively from the previous highest order number in the file.

Booksellers' reports, after they are read into the machine and checked `for accuracy, are sorted by order number and added to the corresponding order records.

Each record corresponding to a book that is still on order is tested to see whether the book ought to have arrived. This testing is based on the assumption that books published in one's own country will be supplied more quickly than those published abroad and that, roughly speaking, the time taken to receive a book is proportional to the distance it has to be sent. A British library might use the following parameters in this test.

Periods within which books should be received

Books published in the U.K. (including books from U.S. publishers with agents in the U.K.)	3 weeks
Books published in Europe	1 month
Books published in the U.S.A.	3 months
Books published elsewhere	3 months

Where a book is discovered to be overdue a "chaser" is printed. This is to remind the bookseller that the book has not arrived and might ask him to report why this is so. The order system must be so designed so that chasers are not printed for books which have arrived in the library since the last computer run. It is also advisable for the librarian to make a quick check on the list of chasers, just in case the machine has made a blunder. It is the ridiculous blunder, when the computer is just beginning to display here something which might be called intelligence, that brings automation into disrepute – and, incidentally, furnishes the raw material for jokes and cartoons.

Information which has been received since the last processing run is used to complete the order record, and if accession numbers have already been added manually this is one point where they can be added to the order record. The estimated price which was included in the record when it was first added to the file is now replaced by the exact price which is being charged to the library. This now includes the effects of discount and postage. It is useful too if the time taken for the order to be received is calculated and included in the record. This will enable statistical analyses to be made later of the actual times it has taken to receive books from various parts of the world. These can be used to modify the parameters which determine when chasers are to be sent, thus enabling the system to improve its performance by experience.

The real advantage of processing slips is that they can save cataloguer's time by carrying bibliographic data from the order system over into the cataloguing process. The same result can be achieved, of course, if the bookseller returns with the book a copy of the original order that was sent to him. This can readily contain full bibliographic information even though the bookseller may not need it. All this is based on the assumption that ordering information is very similar to cataloguing information, can easily be converted into a catalogue record, and so is useful to the cataloguer. It is a very debatable point whether this is true even on the level of manual systems; it depends, in fact, on how fussy the cataloguing department is, on how ready they are to accept the work of the acquisitions department, and on the quality of the bibliographic information available at the time of ordering.

Future of Ordering Data

A further factor arises when the ordering and cataloguing systems are automated. If ordering data can be converted into a catalogue record with only a minimum amount of addition and alteration, then it becomes feasible to make a machine-readable processing slip as well as a legible one. The former can be made into a machine-readable catalogue record without re-keyboarding all of the record. Again, this is perfectly satisfactory where the alterations are minimal, but severe difficulties arise when substantial changes are involved and when the cataloguing department is fussy about the quality of its catalogue.

If the library has implemented a computer-aided circulation system which incorporates mechanical collection of charging data, then the book cards needed for this can conveniently be made at this stage and inserted into the books along with the processing slips. Each book card must be punched with the accession number and the author and title in abbreviated form, and there is little in this which can be made the subject of debate on the grounds of pure cataloguing principles.

A very useful feature of an automated ordering and accessions system is that it can easily include within its scope the production of the library's accessions register. This is printed as a growing series of weekly supplements. Whether accession numbers are assigned to books by the machine or manually, the week's newly accessioned books are simply listed in accession number order. The bookseller who supplied the item, the time taken for the order to be filled, and the date the book was received in the library, etc. Alternatively, this full information may be put in the shelf list record leaving only a brief entry in the accessions register. This eliminates the production of two bulky sequences of records for the library's collection.

Accurate and thorough control of a library's accounts is one of the more valuable services provided by an automated order system. Where each new order is recorded as being charged to a particular account it is a straightforward matter for the computer to encumber the account for the appropriate amount, i.e. record that the library has committed itself to spending that sum. When the book arrives in the library the encumbrance is removed and the net price actually deducted from the fund's real balance.

The machine system can therefore provide a weekly statement of accounts, typically arranged under the following headings:

Fund name		Fund code	
Total spent	Total remaining	Total committed	Total remaining unspent & uncommitted
B	A – B	C	A – (B + C)

where A is the original book grant for the fund, B the total amount actually spent, and C the amount encumbered or committed to be spent. Allowing a percentage for orders which will not be fulfilled, the amount in the right-hand column, A - (B + C), is the balance really remaining in the account.

It is a fairly simple matter to produce any other financial statements which may be required. For example, it may be necessary to compile periodic statements showing the general overall behaviour of the various funds during a particular period, perhaps for the information of senior management. Weekly accounts would be too detailed for such a broad overview. Alternatively, a listing may be required by the bursar's department either showing the net cost of each order and the bookseller who supplied it or giving a monthly listing of orders filled by each bookseller and the total amount to be paid to him. There are many variations possible on this theme of financial reporting.

Statistical System

The possibility of deriving a number of useful statistical analyses from the operation of a computer-aided ordering and accounting system has already been mentioned. It is very easy to compile statistics from a working computer system, so easy, in fact, that there is a great tendency to overdo things and collect a multitude of useless figures along with the ones that really are useful. Statistics can serve two main purposes in a library; they can indicate in quantitative terms what the library has been doing in the past, thus fulfilling an archival function; and they can also provide information to enable the librarian to improve the library's service in the future. These two functions of statistics are, of course, interrelated to a certain degree. For example, a straightforward count of the number of books purchased each year since the library was founded, although primarily a record of the past and interesting and useful as such, can also be used to show the library's growth rate and, possibly, the way the growth rate can be expected to change in the future.

Librarians are notoriously given to counting the things they do. Librarianship possesses a number of humdrum, routine jobs, and it may be that a job becomes less humdrum if one counts the number of times it is done. And then, if one makes all kinds of interesting statistical analyses of the counting, the job becomes positively exciting. A librarian charge of an automated library must decide wisely what he is to count and what he is to forget so as to maximize the effectiveness of the machine time devoted to counting and analysing.

Acquisitions

A number of totals are clearly essential; the total number of acquisitions and, breaking this down, the total number of monographs, pamphlets, gifts, second-hand books, microforms, and other special types of material. The total number of items bought from each of the library's several funds will also be useful. The average costs of the different kinds of material are also valuable. For example, to know how the price of the average physics monograph bought by the library has changed in the past will help to decide what funds to allocate to physics books in the future. If it is found that their cost is increasing more rapidly than the average cost of books on mathematics, say, then proportionately more money must be allocated to physics in order to keep the desired balance between the two subjects. This example of comparative average costs can easily be realized in an automated system, whereas it would be virtually impossible with a manual system. The calculations can be broken down into more detail, by type of material and by source. The library can then optimize its ordering process by ordering from each bookseller the kinds of material he is best able to supply. For example, from bookseller A the library might order all biology books, from bookseller B books about railways. C might be best at supplying maps, microforms, or material from a particular foreign country, and so on. The important point is that these special aptitudes will have been determined experimentally. Furthermore, the system can continue to monitor booksellers' performances because it is conceivable that these might alter through time.

A number of reports can be produced by the system for the benefit of departments within the organization of which the library is a part. These are especially valuable where these departments make recommendations for books to be purchased for the library. Typically, such reports include lists of books proposed by the department that are still on order indicating any relevant booksellers' reports, any books that are unobtainable, and those that have recently arrived in the library. This last kind of list is essentially a list of recent accessions and, of course, most manual systems provide this too. However, the machine system can facilitate the selective dissemination of information about recent accessions, and this is usually more convenient than a blanket listing.

A proposal to buy a book is received from a particular department. The book is ordered and the order record is incorporated into the main machineable order file. The bookseller reports back that the book is out of print. (This is only one of the total number of possible booksellers' reports; all are added to the machine order file but some are also communicated to the originating department, as in the case here.) In this case the department feels that the book is important enough to warrant searching for it on the second-hand market and reports this back to the library. At the next computer processing run the order record is removed from the order file and added to the machine desiderata file, which is also printed.

14

CIRCULATION THROUGH COMPUTERS

The system analyst/programmer has to understand the problems and plan how he should get the information from circulation database to personnels of library and information centres.

Afterwards the programmer, who wants to develop the application software, has to study the following steps:

(a) Prepare decision-making flow chart to problem planned by the system analyst.

(b) Prepare the coded form instruction.

(c) Test the programme until he gets; the correct result.

(d) Pre-detailed documentation of the programme and instructions on its operation.

The programmer has to understand the above steps and prepare the coded instructions which,. the computer understands.

```
*SET TALK OF
*USE LIBCIRI
*CHOICE / 0
*DO WHILE CHOICE / 13
*CLEAR
*TEXT
1. CALL No.
2. AUTHOR
```

```
  3. Jt. AUTHOR
  4. TITLE
  5. ACCESS No.
  6. ISS DATE
  7. DATE DUE
  8. B.T. No.
  9. NAME, ADD
 10. RESERVE 1
 11. ADD NEW DATA DAILY
 12. EDIT
 13. EXIT
 *END TFXT
 *INPUT "GOOD MORNING Reader CHOOSE THEABOVE
OPTION"
 TO CHOICE
 *IF CHOICE =1
 STORE "CALL NO" TO DBP
 *ENDIF
 * IF CHOICE = 2
 *STORE "AUTHOR" DBP
 *ENDIF
 *IF CHOICE = 3
 *STORE "Jt. AUTHOR" TO DBP
 *ENDIF
 *IF CHOICE=4
 *STORE"TITLE" TO DBP
 *ENDIF
 *IF CHOICE = 5
 *STORE "ACCESS NO" TO DBP
 *ENDIF
 *IF CHOICE = 6
 *STORE "ISS DATE" TO DBP
 *ENDIF
 *IF CHOICE = 7
```

```
*STORE "DATE DUE" TO DBP
*ENDIF
*IF CHOICE = 8
*STORE "BTNO" TO DBP
*ENDIF
*IF CHOICE = 9
*STORE "NAME, ADD" TO DBP
*ENDIF
*IF CHOICE = 10
*STORE "RESERVE" TO DBP
*ENDIF
*IF CHOICE =11
*APPEND
*LOOP
*ENDIF
*IF CHOICE = 12
*BROWSE
*LOOP
*ENDIF
*IF CHOICE = 13
*CLEAR
*RETURN
*ENDIF
*CLEAR
*ACCEPT "TYPE ME WHICH and DBP" TO PATIL
*GO TOP
*DO WHILE .NOT. EOP ()
*IF WHICH & DBP = PATIL
*? CALL No. AUTHOR, TITLE, ACCESS No. DATE DUE B.T.
No. OVER DUE, RESERVE 1
*?
*?
*ENDIF
*SKIP
```

```
*END DO
*WAIT
*END DO
*RETURN
```

After the above coded instruction is typed through dBASE III Plus language on the computer screen in order to save it, we have to hold "control and W" which is available on keyboard by hand.

After the above coded instruction is typed you will get the following Menu on your computer screen—

1. CALL No.
2. AUTHOR
3. Jt. AUTHOR
4. TITLE
5. ACCESS No.
6. ISS DATE
7. DATE DUE
8. B.T. No.
9. NAME ADD
10. RESERVE 1
11. ADD NEW DATA DAILY
12. EDIT
13. EXIT

With the above menu the personnel of library and information centres can be approached through different options. They chose the relevant option from the MENU.

Each of the option offered in a MENU consists of; a single number called the "option identifier" (e.g. 4) followed by an explanatory text called the "option description", e.g., if a reader asks the personnel "whom this book has been issued?". .The personnel just select the option 4; the computer is asked to type title, when typing is over the personnel again presses the entry and gets other details as shown below:

CALL No., AUTHOR NAME, TITLE, ACCESS No., DATE DUE, B.T.No. OVER DUE, RESERVE 1. about the book etc.

If a reader bungs only ACCESSION No. of a particular book "shall I know to whom this access No. book has been issued?" the personnel try entering the No.6 option.

After the number is entered the computer is asked to type brought by the reader and the computer sends the following information:

CALL No., AUTHOR, TITLE, ACCESS No., DATE DUE, B.T.No. OVER DUE, RESERVE 1. about the book.

If the book is not issued and computer sends the message `not available' then the personnel try through different approaches to search the information needed by the readers as well as the personnel.

If the personnel want to add new data as how many books are issued per day they have to just enter the number 11 only; they get a `blank space' to add new data to circulation database file.

15

National Policy for Information System

Introduction

Ranganathan suggested that the Imperial Library, Calcutta, might be recognized as the National Central Library, which should be a deposit library for receiving a copy of all Indian publications and also a copyright, library for receiving a second copyright copy of any book published anywhere in India. It should not lend books to readers directly but do so to any primary library on the recommendation of the provincial central library. The proposed National Central Library would thus serve as the apex library of the Indian library system. The library edifice of post-war India should be so planned that primary libraries are attached to regional centres, those in their turn to provincial central libraries, these again to the national central library and this finally to the national central libraries of other countries and international library centres.

- number of unfilled requests by title and quantitative reasons;
- medium of request transmission (e.g., phone) by client type;
- anticipated revenue by payment type (coupon, cash, or free).

The Medical Documentation Services (MDS) division of the library was established in 1953 to provide patrons with specialized information services. The services offered initially consisted of current awareness, indexing, abstracting, and translating. Later, more traditional library programs, such as document delivery, were added to provide MDS clients with a full range of services.

Because each division provides unique and separate information services, the Library Document Delivery Services and MDS divisions enter data using their own versions of the program. At present, Library Document Delivery Services produces a monthly report of document delivery activity. The MDS division plans to produce a comprehensive services report that includes fifty-two sample days of document delivery activity. Future plans include copying subsets of each database for the reporting month and merging these datasets to form a Library/MDS document delivery dataset. Merged reports for the two departments are planned to assess use by title, for purposes of acquisitions, de-accessing, and general collection analysis.

Background: Library Document Delivery Services Division

Each year Library Document Delivery Services receives approximately 35,000 to 40,000 requests. In 1987 the staff began searching for a way in which to streamline statistical processing. Statistics were compiled manually by a full-time paraprofessional on a daily basis. This person was primarily responsible for tallying the number of requests for each borrower and determining the processing status of each request. A report identifying payments anticipated for filled requests was submitted to the library administration each month.

Previous automation efforts in the Library Document Delivery Services used the Powerbase software Program mounted on an IBM PC/AT personal computer with a 30-megabyte hard disk drive. These efforts were an important first step in consolidating delivery statistics from a variety of user groups.

Although the Powerbase software application was available to produce reports for borrower profiles and request processing status, only fifty-two random days each year were designated to sample the use of the collection. The paraprofessional entered data from requests received on these sample days into an Add-record program using this small-scale database. Reports identified the number of requests that were received for individual journal titles on collective sample days. Manual tallying of requests for daily logs (which were necessary for income statistics) and duplicate data entry on these sample days proved excessive. Despite efforts to increase the number of sample days, the Powerbase program could not effectively replace daily logs for a variety of reasons.

Despite the design of a friendly data entry screen, entry and exit from the Add-record program required a thorough understanding of the software. Therefore, data entry was not performed by the document delivery clerks who were responsible for processing the requests. In addition, each Powerbase Add-record screen was lengthy, requiring the paraprofessional to enter of minimum of sixteen fields.

Editing, correcting errors, and updating look-up files required continued, centralized maintenance because the Add-record program did not include error-checking routines. Given the volume of activity end the number of errors, database maintenance tasks conflicted with data entry activities. The lack of error-checking routines was most exasperating when upper and lower case characters were inconsistently entered into data fields.

OBJECTIVES

The library administration defined four broad objectives for the automation of the Library Document Services Division: daily data collection rather than fifty-two random days each year; collection of data at the library clerk revel; regular maintenance of master files and the central database with minimal interruption to daily data entry activities; and the standardization of data collection methods and reports between the document delivery operations of this division and MDS.

To give shape to his ideas, Ranganathan had drafted a Model Public Libraries Act in 1930, which was finally modified by him in 1972. His ideas influenced the Public. Libraries Acts of several states including Tamil Nadu (1948), Andhra Pradesh (1960) and Karnataka (1965). Even the Model Union Public Libraries Bill (1966) of the then Ministry of Education adopted many features of Ranganathan's Model Union Public Libraries Act.

In addition to Public Libraries Acts, Ranganathan also suggested the enactment of a Union Libraries Act for developing a system of

National Central Libraries. Ranganathan is reported to have submitted a memorandum along with a draft Union Library Bill to a committee of the Ministry of Education in 1948. This memorandum and draft bill was published by the University of Delhi in 1950 as 'Library Development Plan: Thirty Years Programme for India'. A refined version of the bill was published in the second edition of Ranganathan's Five Laws of Library Science in 1957. The systems of National Central Libraries, National Service Libraries and the Model Union Libraries Act also formed part of the seminar on Public Library System, 1972, and is included in the book Public Library System.

Ranganathan reiterated the characteristics of a National Central Library in his Library Development Plan. It would organize inter-library loans not only with Indian libraries but also with major international libraries. Departmental libraries should be federated with the National Central Library. It would produce the National Bibliography with different periodicity such as weekly list, monthly bulletin, annual catalogue, decennial catalogue and so on.

The Model Union Library Act of Ranganathan has the following important features:

1. The Union Minister of Education shall be the National Library Authority.
2. He or she will promote and stimulate a state grid of public library system.
3. The system of National Central Libraries will include National Copyright Library, National Dormitory Library and systems of National Service Libraries, National Seafarers Libraries and National Contact Libraries.
4. There shall be a National Department of Libraries with necessary staff.
5. The minister shall appoint the National Librarian for a period of 5 years from among the librarians of National Service Libraries by rotation.
6. There shall be a National Committee of Librarians to discuss problems of common interest.

Early Government Initiatives

Following independence the Government of India took a series of steps to improve library services in the country. The Imperial

Library, Calcutta, was renamed as National Library, India, by the National Library of India (change of name) Act, 1948. Secondly, the UNESCO-sponsored Delhi Public Library was established in 1951 as a model public library. Thirdly, in order to promote documentation services for scientific and industrial research, the Indian National Scientific Documentation Centre (INSDOC) was established in 1952. Fourthly, financial assistance was given to the state governments under the 'scheme of Improvement of Library Services' to set up State Central Libraries and District Libraries during the First Five Year Plan and Second Five Year Plan. Fifthly, in 1954 the Government of India enacted the Delivery of Books (Public Libraries) Act which was amended in 1956 to include newspapers also.

Library Advisory Committee Report

But the most important step was the setting up of an Advisory Committee for Libraries by the Ministry of Education in 1957 under the chairmanship of K.P. Sinha, Director of Public Instruction, Bihar, to recommend suitable measures for the improvement of library services in the country. The Sinha Committee submitted its report in November 1958, and the Report of the Advisory Committee for Libraries was first published in 1959. The important recommendations of the committee may be indicated here.

1. Library service should be free to every citizen of India.
2. The library pattern in the country should consist of the National Library, State central libraries, district libraries, block libraries and panchayat libraries.
3. Every State should have a state library consisting of two wings- the State Central Library and the State Lending Library.
4. At the All-India level, there should be a National Central Library and three National Book Deposit Centres. The National Book Deposit Centres should be run by the Government of India under the National Central Library.
5. There should be an All-India Library Advisory Council with the Union education minister as chairman.
6. Library associations are essential to the development of a library movement, and State Governments and the Government of India should encourage development of strong library associations.

7. Libraries should encourage the formation of Mitra Mandals (Friends of Library Societies) wherever possible.
8. Every state or region should have a centre (Dormitory Library) where books weeded out from the public libraries are sent.
9. Public libraries in the country should cooperate with one another as well as with subscription libraries, school libraries, college libraries, departmental and research libraries, university libraries, and so on. In places where it may not be possible to run an independent public library, school libraries may serve the public after school hours.
10. State governments should accept the responsibility of public library service in their arias. The librarians of these libraries should be State Government employees.
11. Courses for training of professional librarian should be organised by the universities, State Governments or the National Central Library. No university should fun semi-professional courses. They should be run by library associations or by the State Government through the State Library.
12. State Governments should enact a comprehensive State Library Law which will provide for (a) free public library service; (b) a library rate of 6 paise in a rupee of property tax; (c) matching assistance by the State Government to the local bodies.
13. Suitable existing subscription libraries should continue to receive aid from State Governments. The existing subscription libraries should be encouraged to join the proposed free public library service in every. state. New subscription libraries should not be given grants-in-aid. By the end of the Sixth Plan the entire public library system should become free.
14. The Government of India and State Governments should have a 25-year library plan to raise the library structure which will do justice to the cultural and educational needs of the people.
15. The Government of India should enact a library law incorporating (a) the right of every citizen to have free access to library as his fundamental right; (b) collating the various deposit sections under the Copyright Act, Delivery of Books Act and the Press and Registration of Books Act and making them subserve the needs of a National Library Service, end (c) providing for financial assistance to State governments.

On analysis of the recommendations it is evident that the Library Advisory Committee accepted many ideas of Ranganathan, such as free and integrated library service, library legislation both for the State Governments and the Union Government, collection of library cess, constitution of Central Library Advisory Committee and so on. But there is a vital difference of opinion on the nature of deposit law. Though Ranganathan favoured deposit of two copies of a publication in the National Library, under the Copyright Act, he did not oppose the Delivery of Books Act; the criticized the provision for compulsory deposit of foul copies of a publication in four deposit libraries. It also appears that the Library Advisory Committee did not accept Ranganathan's far-sighted recommendation for National Library Systems. On the other hand, it rejected some of his impractical ideas like National Seafarers Library, National Contact Library and National Librarian by rotation. As a sequel to the Report of the Library Advisory Committee, the Union Ministry of Education circulated a Model Public Libraries Bill in 1966. Almost simultaneously, the Working Group on Libraries set up by the Planning Commission for the Fourth Five Year Plan submitted a report including a Model Public Libraries Bill; but it has little significance for a national library policy.

RRRLF

The next important step was the establishment of Raja Rammohun Roy Library Foundation in 1972 as an autonomous organization under the Department of Culture, Government of India. One of the principal objectives of the Foundation is to enunciate a national library policy and to work towards its adoption by the Central and State Governments.[1] This is the first explicit commitment of the Government of India for adoption of a national library policy.

International Developments

A wind of change was blowing over the field of library and information services since 1960s. We may cite some of these important developments here:

1. In the United Kingdom the British government adopted a new Public Libraries and Museums Act in 1964, ensuring involvement of the government in the provision of library

services by the local bodies. Another important landmark is the establishment of the British Library in 1972 by the amalgamation of several important libraries of England.

2. In the United States of America, the federal government set up by an Act a National Commissioner on Libraries and Information Science in 1970 on the recommendation of the National Advisory Commission on Libraries.
3. UNESCO gave a new thrust to the library and information sector in 1970s. It promoted World Scientific Information System (UNISIST) and National Information System (NATIS) and implemented them through the General Information Programme (PGI). The three major inter governmental conferences: UNISIST I, NATIS and UNISIST II were organized in 1971, 1974 and 1979 respectively. It disseminated new ideas and policy matters through bulletins, monographs, manuals, handbooks, standards and guidelines, training manuals and packages, reports, seminar proceedings, project documents, and so on. In the context of national library and information policy the following may be mentioned as important documents: (a) Information Policy Objectives, 1974; (b) Guidelines on the Planning of National Scientific and Technological Information Systems, 1975; (c) Planning National Information Structures for Documentation, Libraries and Archives: Outline of General Policy, 1975.
4. The International Federation of Library Associations and Institutions (IFLA), founded in T929, stepped up its activities during this period. Its programme of Universal Bibliographic Control, Universal Availability of Publications and International MARC received substantial support from UNESCO and generated wide interest in the library world.
5. The development of Global Information Systems (like International Nuclear Information Systems [INIS], Agricultural Information System [AGRIS]) and of International Databases in subject fields offering on-line searches to users. all over the world (such as Chemical Abstracts by Chemical Abstracts Service, USA, MEDLARS by National Medical Library, USA) greatly contributed to the promotion of information infrastructure in many parts of the world.

NISSAT

The establishment of the National Information System for Science and Technology (NISSAT) in 1977 was the first important step taken by the Department of Science and Technology, Government of India, to develop a well-conceived library and information system for promoting research in science and technology.

Professor R.K. Das Gupta's Advocacy

The National Library of India (Amendment) Act was passed in 1976. It provided for the creation of an autonomous National Library Board. Professor R.K. Das Gupta was appointed the first director under the act, though the act has been kept under suspension. In 1977 he wrote to the Government of India urging the appointment of a National Library Advisory Commission to advise the government in respect of a national library policy and a national library system. According to Professor Das Gupta, The National Library can function as a National Library proper, that is, as a library for the serious investigator or a library of last resort only when there is a sound library system in the country. For a sound library system we need a library policy and that policy has w be enunciated by the Central Government.' Since Professor Das Gupta's proposal found no response from the Government of India, he urged the Raja Rammohun Roy Library Foundation (RRRLF) to take up the task in terms of the principal objectives of its Memorandum of Association.

RRRLF Initiative

Professor Das Gupta became the chairman of the Raja Rammohun Roy Library Foundation from November 1979 to August 1981. At his instance the RRRLF organized a series of lectures on different aspects of library service by some eminent library scientists of the country during 1981. 'The lectures were published as Indian Libraries : Trends and Perspectives (Orient Longman, Calcutta, 1985). The Foundation also took a memorable decision, at its meeting held on 22 May 1981, to draft a national library policy, and the Chairman was authorized to appoint a working group consisting of three to five persons who possessed wide knowledge and experience in library administration or education. In pursuance of this decision he appointed a working group consisting of the following persons:

1. Professor R.K. Das Gupta--Chairman
2. Professor P.B. Mangla
3. Shri S. Biswas
4. Professor K.A.Issac
5. Dr. B.P. Barua – Convener

No terms of reference were prescribed. The working group was only required to draft a national library policy for the consideration of the Foundation. Prof. Das Gupta could not, however, attend any meeting of the working group.

At its first meeting the working group decided the scope of the policy as follows:

(a) The policy should be called 'National Policy on Library and Information System' to avoid any possibility of confusion.

(b) The policy should be comprehensive? It should include all categories of libraries-national, public, academic and special (including research, government departmental and manuscript libraries) but excluding museums and archives.

(c) All aspects of librarianship: bibliographic control, library and information science education, library legislation, library cooperation, information technology and so on should be covered in the national policy.

IASLIC and ILA Conference

The Indian Association of Special Libraries and Information Centres (IASLIC) organized their eleventh and twelfth conference on the themes relevant to national library and information policy. The theme of the Eleventh IASLIC Conference held at Dharwar, Karnataka, in 1977, was 'Planning of National Information Network', and that of the Twelfth IASLIC Conference held at Roorkee in 1979 was 'National Information Policy'. Similarly, the Indian Library Association (ILA) discussed, 'National Library and Information Policy' at the Thirteenth. All-India Library Conference held at Jaipur in 1984. Some of the papers contributed in these conferences added greatly to the crystallization of ideas and thoughts on the projected national policy on library and information systems. On behalf of the

Indian Library Association a draft policy statement was submitted to the Government of India in early 1985.

Planning Commission

The Planning Commission brought out the Report of the Working Group on Modernization of Library Services and Informatics for the Seventh Five Year Plan in 1984. The report is divided into two parts-the first part dealt with library services and the second part outlined the informatics developmental activities. The document presents many ideas with particular reference to development of information technology and its application in library and information services in India.

CONPOLIS

The Department of Culture, Government of India set up a Committee on National Policy on Library and Information System (CONPOLIS) on 7 October 1985 under the chairmanship of Professor D.P. Chattopadhyaya, Chairman, RRRLF. The committee included some eminent library scientists and educationists of the country: B.S. Kesavan, Ashin Das Gupta, Girija Kumar, T.S. Rajagopalan, K.A. Issac, B. Anderson, P.B. Mangla, P.N. Kaula, Suseela Kumar, S.C. Biswas, Y. Rajaraman, R.C. Tripathi, B.D. Nag Chowdhury, Ravinder Kumar and B.P. Barua (Member-Secretary). CONPOLIS had the following terms and conditions:

To consider the document `National Policy on Library and Information System' prepared ay the Raja Rammohun Roy Library Foundation in the context of an expanding library movement, disseminating information of neo-literates, illiterates, children and backward communities. The committee may also consider a document on a national policy prepared by the Indian Library Association.

(a) To circulate these documents to relevant experts and institutions all over the country and determine their reaction;

(b) To arrange a public discussion on the policy statement by way of holding seminars or by conducting interviews of selected people;

(c) On the basis of its own discussions of the documents and on the basis of public reactions as determined through (b) and (c) the committee should prepare a final document for the consideration of the government.

CONPOLIS held its first meeting on 9-10 December 1985 and the last meeting on 14-15 February 1986 in Calcutta. The members of the committee toured different parts of the country jointly and severally to exchange views with cross sections of the people. Comments were invited and received from several organizations, institutions and individuals. An interim report was submitted by the chairman on 8 March 1986. It highlighted the role of libraries in the New Education Policy. The final report, 'National Policy on Library and Information System: A Presentation' was submitted to the Minister of Human Resource Development on 30 May 1986. The fate of the CONPOLIS Report is not known. But it is learnt that an Empowered Committee set up by the Department of Culture examined the Report and submitted its comments in March 1988. An implementation cell has since been set up. However, the Government of India has yet to formally accept the recommendations contained in the documents.

16

National Information System for Science and Technology

INFORMATION AND ITS NEEDS

Information Defined

Before an in-depth discussion on the current activities and the projected plans of NISSAT could be undertaken, it is necessary to understand the changing role of information. Acquisition of scientific and technical documents or publishing a number of bibliographies by themselves could not be called 'information' activities. Nor can publication of directories and results of survey alone be claimed to be 'information' chores.

'Information' must be distinguished from data. 'Data' whether it is numeric or bibliographic, relates to facts, figures, or recorded documents expressed in the form of symbols. But in order that data may qualify to become 'information' it should be processed, organised, and presented to a person or agency at the time needed for taking some action. Thus information embraces three important characteristics of timeliness, person affiliation and action orientation.

Scientific and technological information, thus, in the conventional sense, refers to the type of information that pertains to research activities usually in the natural and social sciences. It also includes, according to the main working, document of UNISIST II, 'knowledge necessary in the technical and managerial fields to produce goods and services needed by society.'

How to Measure Information

Information, by its very nature, could be very effective for one group while not being so for another. But before one sets out to assess the effectiveness of information, some means must be evolved to measure the content of information. A number of learned articles have been written on this aspect, but as yet no concrete methodology has been evolved. Added to this uncertainty about the unit of measurement is the fact that the giver or 'generator' of information may lose nothing at all in tangible terms by parting with information and the recipient may not gain much by receiving a piece of information. Hence, the need to associate action orientation with information so that if no action is taken by the recipient, no information could be said to have been communicated., Such a 'null' hypothesis aids in some small measure towards studying the content of information.

With the aforementioned theoretical concepts, we may now venture into areas of design and development of an information system. It is perhaps, easier to identify problem areas in the fields of science and technology mainly because of the presence of an organised, articulating group of target audience. But even here, one justifiably can and does ask as to what is so particular now, that so much attention be paid to information systems and their development.

The Need for an Information System

It is an acknowledged fact that the three principal factors that demand the establishment of a well-organised system relate to, firstly, the growth in the output of scientific and technical literature; secondly; the increasing influence speedy sharing of such information has on the generation of new ideas; and thirdly, the role such transfer of information plays in converting a discovery into a device. It would augur well to briefly consider these aspects.

Growth of Scientific and Technical Literature

There is no gainsaying the fact that the output of scientific and technological literature has grown to huge proportions. The trend of growth in different subjects is shown in tables. As can be seen from the table, it is no longer possible for information specialists to keep track of such literature with the help of conventional tools alone. Whatever be the nature of the country (developed or developing), recourse to computer-resident databases appears to be the answer if one were to keep apprising the user community the latest developments in science and technology.

Table 16.1. World Output of Scientific and Technical Articles in Periodicals

Subject	Approximate number of articles		
	1960	1970 (estimated)	1980 (estimated)
Mathematics	15,000	30,000	50,000
Physics	75,000	1,55,000	2,30,000
Engineering	1,55,000	2,75,000	
	--------------	--------------	
Civil	15,000	15,000	30,000
Mechanical	10,000	20,000	40,000
Elelctrical Engineering	80,000	1,50,000	4,00,000
Aerospace	35,000	75,000	1,50,000
Industrial	15,000	15,000	30,000
Chemistry	1,50,000	2,80,000	5,00,000
Metallurgy	35,000	50,000	1,00,000
Biology	1,50,000	2,60,000	4,00,000
Geoscience	91,000	1,58,000	4,00,000
Agriculture	1,50,000	2,60,000	5,00,000
Medicine	2,20,000	3,90,000	6,00,000
Psychology	15,000	30,000	50,000
Other Subjects	9,29,000	18,82,000	25,00,000
Total	**19,85,000**	**37,80,000**	**59,00,000**

Generation of New Ideas

The increasing tempo of activities in the publication of scientific and technical discoveries and achievements gives rise, in turn, to generation of new ideas. Publications have a 'multiplier effect' and this is reflected by the large scale increase in the creation of new ideas in the different fields of science and technology in the twentieth century as compared to previous centuries. Table 16.2 reveals such growth. Such a thrust in the generation of new ideas has been possible because of the free exchange of information between scientists and technologists with no concern whatever for traditional geographic and national boundaries.

Table 16.2. Major New Ideas during Different Periods

	Number of new ideas and subjects created		
Main Subject	**1451-1700 (250 years)**	**1701-1900 (200 years)**	**1901-1950 (50 years)**
Mathematics	9	24	21
Physics	3	21	63
Engineering	1	23	46
Chemistry	0	36	80
Technology	0	21	70
Bio logy	2	4	8
Geology	1	16	8
Botany	1	7	4
Agriculture	0	2	2
Zoology	0	4	4
Medicine	4	21	80
Total	**21**	**180**	**391**

Bridging of Discovery-to-device Gap

A major by-product of scientific discoveries is the production of appliances and devices to serve the needs of the society at large. Here again, information acts as a crucial catalyst in bridging the gap between discovery-to-device time-lag. This is evident from a perusal of Table 16.3 which reflects the shortening of time duration between a discovery and its conversion to a device in different applications. We may attribute the shortening of this gap to faster and freer flow of information between the research scientist on the one hand and the production units on the other.

Table 16.3. Time Lag between Discovery-to-device

Sl. No.	Invention	Year of Discovery/	Development of device or use	Time lag between discovery and development (in years)
1.	Internal Combustion Engine	1710	1892	182
2.	Photography	1727	1839	112
3.	Aerial Flight	1809	1903	94
4.	Telephone	1823	1876	53
5.	Radar	1899	1935	48
6.	Gamma Ray	1896	1939	43
7.	Atomic Power Release	1932	1945	13
8.	Transistor	1940	1948	8
9.	Laser	1958	1960	2

The Indian Scenario

In the evolution of any system, let alone information system, one of the foremost activities is to identify the user community, both current and potential. Since the National Information System for Science & Technology (NISSAT) started with the aim of meeting the information needs of scientists and technologists in India, let us dwell a little on this type of user community. The number of scientific and technical personnel in India was estimated to be 2.3 million in 1977.6 These scientists and technologists normally work in research laboratories and institutions which number about 350 (when all types of institutions are counted). Concomitant with the establishment of research laboratories, the expenditure on scientific research has been stepped up from a sum of Rs. 47 million in 1950-51 to approximately Rs. 4,000 million in 1976-77. This figure, however, when seen as a percentage of GNP shows it only as 0.6 per cent as is evident from Table 16.4.

Table 16.4. Percentage of GNP devoted to R and D in Some Countries

0 to 0.5%		0.5 to 1.0%		1 to 2%		2 to 3%	
Pakistan	0.2 (73)	Argentina	0.5 (74)	Australia	1.0 (73)	UK	2.0 (72)
Mexico	0.2 (71)	India	0.6 (76_77)	Sweden	1.6 (73)	FRG	2.1 (73)
Spain	0.3 (74)	Ghana	0.9 (72)	Canada	1.7 (73)	USA	2.3 (74)
Korea	0.4 (74)	Italy	0.9 (74)	France	1.7 (74)	Japan	2.5 (75)
						Poland	2.7 (75)

The Emerging Panorama

While conventional information systems, utilising modern devices wherever necessary, are adequate to meet the needs of scientists and technologists, another class of user community is emerging. This class consists of entrepreneur, 'both large-scale and small-scale, professionals, rural population and the public at large. In keeping with the aspirations of the people as highlighted in the plan allocations in India, science and technology is expected to, and justifiably so, become more appealing and popular to the general population. Thus, scientific and technological communication assumes a new dimension, and, increasing emphasis is expected to be laid on information repackaging techniques.

The NISSAT Scheme

One might now ask as to what are the objectives of NISSAT. What has NISSAT accomplished so far? What are its various components? How is it being co-ordinated? What are the priority areas chosen for development? What are the directions in which the NISSAT project is progressing? How would it fit into the overall pattern of a world information network? These are some of the questions, answers to which will be attempted now.

NISSAT Objectives

The NISSAT project as described in Country Report presented by India in the second UNISIST meeting on Planning and

Implementation of National Information Activities$ aims to achieve the following objectives

(a) Provision of national information service relevant to present needs and capable of development to meet the future r.eeds of the generators, processors, disseminators and users of information;

(b) Optimum utilisation of existing information services and systems and the development of new ones ;

(c) Promotion of national and international co-operation and liaison for exchange of information ;

(d) Support and active encouragement for the development of facilities for education and training in information science and technology, and in communication to provide qualified manpower for the implementation of the national science information policy;

The above objectives were expected to be achieved over a 15-year period. The scheme also envisages establishment of new information centres and augmentation of existing ones, wherever possible. The NISSAT project is expected to be built with the support of Sectoral Information Centres at the 'grass-roots' level interlinked by means of Regional Information Centres. The activities of Sectoral Centres and Regional Centres is being coordinated by a Headquarters situated in the Department of Science and Technology of the Government of India in Delhi.

Sectoral Centres and their Roles

While according priority to the establishment of Sectoral Information Centres, one was confronted with the all-important question of, which discipline needed higher priority. Keeping in view the spin-off$ an information subsystem would create in rural development, disciplines like food, leather, drugs and pharmaceuticals and machine tools were chosen in the first instance. A brief description of each of these centres at this juncture would be in order.

Food information center-Foodgrains and food products resulting from post-harvest technology have been seizing the attention of planners in India for quite some time. Even though nearly 330 million hectares of land is under cultivation in India, import of foodgrains (to the extent of 6.5 million tonnes in 1976) continues to be an on-going activity. Attention, therefore, is being focused on discovering new plants and products which would be locally available and yet would prove to be nutritive and appealing. It is in this context that the role of Central Food Technological Research Institute (CFTRI) located at Mysore is considered important. The National Information Centre for Food Science and Technology has been established in CFTRI and is engaged in the collection, storage, organisation, retrieval and dissemination of information relating to food science and technology. With the advent of NISSAT, a thrust has been given to acquisition of more documents, both, in the printed and microform, and publication of fascicules on nutrition, special subjects like mango cultivation, food preservation, etc.

Leather information centre: Leather is another area which merits attention particularly by virtue of its contribution to the growth of rural industries. By motivating tanners, and other entrepreneurs, the Central Leather Research Institute (CLRI) located at Madras has been able to reduce the quantum of export of raw hides and skins and at the same time, increase the quantity of export of finished leather and leather manufactures (excluding footwear) over the years. The export of leather goods was Rs. 258 million in 1950-51 while it increased to Rs. 2,635 million in 1976-77. There has been a corresponding decline in the export of undressed hides and skins from a figure of Rs. 96 million in 1950-51 to Rs. 8 million in 1976-77. The National Information Centre in Leather and Allied Industries (NICLAI) located at CLRI has undertaken to fulfil not only conventional functions but also publish periodicals in Indian languages such as Urdu, Hindi and Tamil. Since the tanning community is not very happy with printed documents alone, efforts are under way to prepare audio-visual aids such as film strips, slides, transparencies, etc. Such as attempt at 'show-how' as opposed to 'know-how' dissemination has found wide acceptance with the user population.

Drugs and pharmaceuticals information center: The existence of the Central Drug Research Institute (CDRI), Lucknow is note worthy as evidenced by the growth in the production of Drug and Pharmaceuticals from Rs. 120 million in 1948 to Rs. 7000 million in 1976-77. The CDRI has been able to synthesise a number of compounds indigenously and also conduct studies on the medicinal plants found in India with a view to determining their composition with regard to known elements such as Potassium, Nitrogen, etc. Nearly 4000 such plants have been analysed by CDRI so far. The National Information Centre for Drugs and Pharmaceuticals (NICMAP) located at CDRI not only caters to the needs of CDRI but also provides information services at the national level with specific reference to manufacturing units, such as the Indian Drugs and Pharmaceuticals Limited and the Hindustan Antibiotics Limited.

Machine tools information center: While food, leather and drugs could be termed consumer sectors ; machine tools sector deals with industrial goods. The Central Machine Tools Institute (CMTI) located at Bangalore is a national institute of excellence which has been increasingly promoting import substitution over the years. The magnitude of the industry can be gauged from the fact that 118 major units produced machine tools worth about Rs. 1130 million in the year 1976-77 and exported machine tools worth about Rs. 180 million in the same year. The National Information Centre for Machine Tools and Allied Products (NICMAP) located in CMTI has been bringing out publications in the machine tools sector on a regular basis. NICMAP, as opposed to other Sectoral Centres, is able to utilise the computing facilities provided at the CMTI Computer Centre equipped with a PDP-II computer.

Contribution of Nissat

With the advent of NISSAT, there has been a greater shift towards streamlining document collection, increasing emphasis on information dissemination activities, an increasing awareness about the need to identify potential users and an urge to meet the needs of users, be they scientists, technologists, small-scale entrepreneurs, or the public at large.

In a recent survey conducted by the author, some of the facts that emerge are:

(i) Whereas the budgetary allocation for the Food Sectoral Centre was of the order of 3 per cent of total GFTRI budget in the pre-NISSAT days, it has increased to nearly 12 per cent with financial inputs from NISSAT ; the corresponding figure for the. Machine Tools Sectoral Centre are 3 per cent of the total

CMTI budget before and 7 per cent after the advent of NISSAT. The figures for other Sectoral centres run on similar lines.

(ii) Such increases in financial inputs seem to have given a much needed fillip to purchase of firstly, equipment like plain paper copiers, microfilm reader printers; secondly, conference proceedings which would otherwise not have been bought, thirdly, essential periodicals and journals, and fourthly, standards and patents whose number keeps increasing day by day.

(iii) In the absence of NISSAT inputs, the number of documents effectively purchased would have decreased because of an increase in the price of publications.

A few other activities of Sectoral Centres that are noteworthy and merit attention are:

(i) Compilation of a Thesaurus for machine tools by the NICMAP.

(ii) Translation activities undertaken by the NICLAI. Publications brought out in Indian languages earlier but were lying dormant have been restarted.

(iii) Publications in the form of Digests with a high content of state-of-the-art articles are being brought out regularly by all the Sectoral Centres.

While every attempt is being made by the Sectoral Centres to provide information service to any person located anywhere in India in the first instance, it becomes necessary to provide some focal points in different regions of the country. These focal points would act as switching centres and route requests from people in the region to the concerned Sectoral Centres.

In any information network, whether it be national or inter national, all the components would not normally be on the pay roll of one single agency. Therefore, the co-ordinating group of such a system has to adopt a management strategy of the laisses faire type. No rigid time frames and regulations can be stipulated nor can one remote-control operations of a Sectoral centre from the Headquarters.

In keeping with the above philosophy, the NISSAT Co-ordinating Group with a very small contingent of staff is engaging itself in some important areas of national relevance. While undertaking such projects, due attention is being paid for evolving norms and standards such that monitoring and evaluation would be facilitated at a later stage. Some of the schemes sponsored centrally by NISSAT Programmes are:

(1) Training programmes;
(2) Publication of directories;
(3) Translation activities;
(4) Standardisation measures;
(5) Machine-readable databases;
(6) Experiment on facsimile transmission; and
(7) Access to international databases through telex.

Training programmes: Manpower development programmes are essential on-going activities aimed at improving the skills of personnel operating the information system. The training imparted need not relate to new skills but may confine itself only to updating the knowledge of the people who might have left the portals; of educational institutions some years earlier. It is with this view that the NISSAT coordinating group has organised a number of country-wide courses and supported seminars and workshops. One course focused attention on 'indexing techniques' while the second dwelt on 'reprographic techniques.' Considering the need for developing management skills of senior personnel of the sectoral estates, a course on 'systems analysis' was also conducted. This course which included topics like system design and implementation, introduction to computers, operations research techniques, usage of machine-readable databases, etc. was found to be very popular. Similar courses are being planned for future also.

Principal among the sponsored seminars and workshops are the seminar on Primary Communications in Science and Technology in India (PRICSTI) held at the Documentation Research and Training Centre (DRTC), at Bangalore and the CODATA Workshop at Bhabha Atomic Research Centre (BARC), Bombay.

Publication of directories: Since its inception, NISSAT has been promoting activities related to inventory of research programmes, testing facilities, etc. The 'Directory of Testing Facilities' is unique in the sense that it acts as a catalyst for the small-scale entrepreneurs for improving the quality of their products by seeking access to the testing facilities close to their factory sites. This is an on-going activity.

The 'Directory of Current Research Projects' which is being prepared currently, is a one-shot activity since the data contained therein are rather volatile. It is, therefore, proposed to store this directory in the form of a magnetic-tape oriented database.

Another important directory which is under compilation relates to inventorising product profiles for small scale industries. There are nearly 0.5 million small scale industrial units in India and many more are yet to be established in keeping with the plans of the Government. Any small-scale entrepreneur looks out for product profiles giving details of type of product he can manufacture at his place, the cost elements involved, availability of marketing channels, etc. Such product profiles have been prepared for a number of products by the Small Scale Service Institute (SIS) established all over India. But there is no consolidated list of such profiles. This directory attempts to meet this need.

Translation activities: In a recent survey conducted on the availability of translators in scientific and technical fields in India for translating from various foreign languages to English, it was found that there were nearly 400 well-qualified translators available. In order to assess the level of competence of those translators, a written test was conducted and only those themselves listed in the directory. Steps are also being taken by NISSAT to promote translation of scientific literature by sectoral centres not only from some foreign languages to English but also from English to a few Indian languages. A survey has also been launched by NISSAT in conjunction with the Indian Scientific Translators Association in order to assess the potential in such areas.

Standardisation measures and committees: With a view to achieving a certain degree of rationalisation and standardisation, the NISSAT co-ordinating group has set up various committees. One such committee is the Manpower Development Committee. This commutes has set out to identify the courses offered by nearly 42. universities in the field of conventional Library Science. Every effort is being made to study the existing syllabi and suggest changes to provide for exposure to handling of reprographic equipment, machine-readable databases, etc.

Another important committee which has been constituted attempts to identify the type of hardware required in the different components of NISSAT programme, and suggest indigenisation wherever possible. In the initial stages, this committee is confining itself to reprographic equipment, such as plain-paper copiers, microfilm/fiche readers and printers, process cameras, etc.

Machine-readable databases: UNESCO had supported an experiment of computer-based Selective Dissemination of Information (SDI) by providing software and training to Indian personnel, in 1976. Since then, the SDI project has been in vogue utilising the IBM-370/155 computer system installed at the Indian Institute of Technology, Madras. Nearly 250 scientists and technologists all over India are being provided SDI service using chemical abstracts database once a fortnight and INSPEC database once a month. An experiment is under way to utilise the COMPENDEX database and this service is expected to commence during 1976 itself. These services are operated through the Indian National Scientific Documentation Centre (INSDOC). The SDI service rendered to the scientists in India is gratis as opposed to international services, such as DIALOG, ORBIT, etc. A proposal is under consideration to levy a nominal fee from the recipients of this service. India has also been contributing to two well-known international information services, such as International Nuclear Information System (INIS) and Agricultural Information System (AGRIS). The INIS input is on paper-tape and on work-sheets sent from the Bhabha Atomic Research Centre (BARC) at Bombay and this process has been in vogue since 1972. For want of adequate computing facility, the INIS magnetic tapes arc not being utilised fully. The AGRIS input from India, on the other hand, commenced in 1976. The AGRIS contact point in India is the Indian Council of Agricultural Research (ICAR) and in this case, information contained in magnetic tapes received from AGRIS is disseminated to about 35 Agricultural Institutes once a month. The Burroughs B4700 computer installed at the Institute of Agricultural Research Statistics (IARS) premises handles the AGRIS database. The computer scientists of IARS have developed retrieval programmes for facilitating quick information retrieval from AGRIS database.

An experiment is also underway to structure the SDI services around an indigenous computing facility by developing appropriate software. As time passes, this service would be able to provide a retrospective search also in addition to current service. While the computer-based SDI service is being provided for internationally available databases, a manual SDI service is being attempted in areas such as leather, where no international service apparently exists. Hopefully, the SDI service would be enlarged to other sectoral applications also and would operate as a distributed network rather than a centralised or star connection. It must be recorded here that it takes time to impress upon the scientific community that information also costs money. Therefore, every attempt is being made to improve the quality of service and at the same time apprise the user community of the fact that information also involves an element of cost primarily because of the effort involved in its collection, organisation, search, retrieval and dissemination.

Experiment on facsimile transmission: Facsimile transmission has been in vogue in India for a number of years, particularly for newspapers, having been introduced in 1969 at Madras facilitating simultaneous printing of a newspaper at Coimbatore, a distance of nearly 500 km. This service was extended to Bangalore in 1970 and is available in Hyderabad also presently. When it comes to the question of extending facsimile facilities of transmission by communication channels for documents, normally one A-4 page transmission would cost anywhere up to Rs. 54/- if one wishes to transmit from Delhi to Bangalore over a distance of about 2,200 km using subscriber trunk dialing facility. Added to this is the nature of P & T Rules, wherein it is stipulated that one will have to pay for a dedicated line while utilising facsimile devices as opposed to telex services.

Accessing international databases through telex: It must be recorded here that UNESCO had supported an experiment in September 1976, in which databases available at Frascati, Rome, could be accessed from a query-type device situated in Bombay. This experiment was very well received by the scientific community and one was hoping to establish such a linkage on a more permanent basis. In order: to create an awareness with regard to the availability of database in EURONET environment and also work out a specific budgetary appropriation, an experiment is underway by which one is seeking recourse to telex channels for communication with one of the terminals of EURONET in Europe. This is purely in an experimental stage and it is hoped that with adequate UNESCO financial assistance, India will be able to provide an on-line service to some of the databases available in Europe in the first instance.

NISSAT — QUO VADIS

The NISSAT project can rightly be said to be in its infancy. It is proposed to launch five more sectoral centres during the coming years after due approval has been obtained from the concerned Government agencies in the all important areas of (i) small industries; (ii) textiles; (iii) chemicals; (iv) minerals; and (v) aeronautics.

Aeronautics particularly has been chosen in preference to other application areas primarily because of a very rich collection of documents in the concerned information centre as well as the advances made in allied disciplines by the National Aeronautics Laboratory, Bangalore. Areas such as roads, oceanography, medicinal plants, tea, rubber, jute, petro-chemicals, glass and ceramics, wood, etc. would be given adequate emphasis as the project gathers momentum.

Computer based information systems: It is proposed to equip the existing sectoral centres on an experimental basis with computers (mainly those made in India) and gradually develop information systems using computers. A plan is also underway to link one of the regional centres to a sectoral centre by means of existing telecommunication channels for exchange of documents and information between the two.

Microfilming of Indian documents – It is hoped to generate microfilms and micro-fiches of documents already available in the various sectoral centres, particularly those relating to research reports which may not be in a printed form.

Facsimile experiments – Facsimile experiments are also being undertaken so that documents could be exchanged through telecommunication channels between different parts of India. Faster scanning and receiving devices with a facility to accommodate bulky books and periodicals, it is hoped, would be developed in the next few years.

Some Useful Lessons

Some of the important lessons that the various personnel of NISSAT during its short existence have learnt can be classified under the following headings

(i) **Need for 'information salesmen':** There appears to be a feeling among the user community that information would be available free of cost and the personnel manning information centres could be relegated to the background since the latter, the user community assumes, provide only responsive service. Perhaps, there is a need to create a breed of 'information salesmen' who would not only report passively through the medium of secondary information products and respond to user requests but also aggressively sell 'information products.' For such a scenario to emerge, the information scientists would have to equip themselves with knowledge and skill more than conventional acquisition and classification skills.

(ii) **Training in management skills:** With the emergence of computer-based databases, and ocher modern techniques, the managers of information centres trained some years ago in conventional library science, find themselves wanting in their ability to manage the centres. Therefore, periodic refresher courses need to be organised for these personnel so that this need could be fulfilled.

(iii) **Costing information products:** Even though information products could be distributed gratis to the target population in the initial stages, the centres marketing such products must work out a pricing strategy such that, in the long run, such services pay for themselves. Many of the welfare schemes continue to be heavily subsidised, and justly so, but information services should gear themselves to being subjected to cost-benefit analysis studies. Perhaps, one might recommend incorporation of membership Fees being levied on the lines of the library-fees. Such membership fees should permit the member to seek access to any database provided by the service, for after all, is not a member of a library entitled to borrow any book (excepting reference books) whatever its cost be?

(iv) **Distributed network more useful compared to over-centralisation:** It has been found that information services should be provided on a distributed basis to cover the length and breadth of the country rather than concentrating them at one place: Such distribution, though problematic from managerial, training and standardisation angles, tend to grow on strong foundations mainly because of participation by a larger population. If centralisation is resorted to, purely based on considerations of efficiency in the initial stages, there is every likelihood. that different regions of the country would not progress equitably in this field. There is bound to be concentration around a few centres of excellence.

(v) **Need for evolving norms in the initial stages:** Even though an information system should be nurtured in its infancy, there is a need to evolve yardsticks and norms in the beginning itself such that the performance of the system could be monitored and evaluated as it progresses. It is in this context that the NISSAT activities being subjected to a review even when it is hardly two years old is a welcome sign.

Role of UNISIST

As the success of the National Information System in India is dependent largely upon its constituent agencies, so also is the realisation of a World Information System possible only with the active participation and co-operation of various member countries of UNESCO. In order to realise such a dream of UNESCO, one would have to take some preliminary steps. Some of these are:

(i) inventorising the activities of and services offered by National Information Systems;

(ii) providing training to personnel of developing countries, on a more regular basis, in areas such as management and administration, modern computing devices, etc.;

(iii) setting norms and standards for the National Information Systems which enter the World Information Network on a time-period basis. In the initial stages of operation, a laissez faire approach is recommended;

(iv) establishing Regional Information Centres of the World Information System in developing countries in order to act as a focal point for that relegion;

(v) arranging meetings of member countries more often, say once in three years, in order to facilitate exchange, of notes among them and ensure balanced progress of the network; and

(vi) offer financial assistance on an increasing scale to developing countries so that purchase of costly equipment for providing modern information services could be facilitated (equipment such as computers, fast reprographic equipment, special purpose word processing machines, etc., could be supplied).

The role played by UNISIST so far is laudable and the foregoing is, not new, but perhaps, an increasing range of activities would enhance the progress towards development of a World Information Network.

Conclusion

Every effort has been made in this paper to analyse the need for scientific and technical information in the first instance. A definition of information as an entity distinct from data has also been attempted. The advent of NISSAT and its growth till date has been traced. It is hoped that in the years to come the progress of NISSAT as a well-organised and established information system would become a reality.

One of the major-problem areas identified during project execution relates to development of skills of personnel manning the different components of the project. The NISSAT Co-ordination Group has accorded a very high priority to this aspect. Meetings with experts of international repute would further enhance fulfilment of this objective.

17

INFORMATION SERVICES OF DESIDOC

Evolution of DESIDOC

At the time of formation of Defence Science Organisation in 1948 information service was confined to the indexing of current literature and building up of Defence Science Library. The scope of service was enlarged with the setting up of Scientific Information Bureau in 1958 which later became the Defence Scientific Information and Documentation Centre (DESIDOC) in 1967. it functioned under the administrative and technical control of Defence Science Laboratory, now called Defence Science Centre. In July 1970, DESIDOC was declared as self-accounting unit and became one of the establishments under the defence R and D Organisation with the following charter of duties:

(i) To function as Scientific Information and Documentation Centre, to cater to the information needs of R and D Headquarters and all R and D Laboratories/Establishments.

(ii) To collect, collate and disseminate scientific and technical information on all aspects of defence science to those entitled to receive such information.

(iii) To act as repository for all technical and research reports of foreign/Indian origin particularly those connected with defence science.

(iv) To maintain close liaison with INSDOC.

(v) To translate literature and reports from foreign languages.

This charter needed revision in the eighties in view of the many changes that have occurred in the national and international scene. A number of developments have taken place in the field of information science and technology resulting in the emergence of new methods and techniques. To meet the present day requirements, the charter of duties of DESIDOC was recently revised and was approved in June 1981. The new charter of duties is as follows:

(i) To function as a central resource for providing scientific information / documentation / library/reprographic/ translation services to the DRDO HQrs/Labs/Estts and to co-ordinate DRDO scientific information programmes.

(ii) To develop a data-bank on scientific information far DRDO and an information .system for Defence Science and Technology and to interface with other national international agencies in the field of scientific information.

(iii) To provide training and user education programmes for DRDO and all defence users and carry out R and D work in the field of scientific information documentation.

(iv) To provide consultancy and referral services to TICS/ Libraries of DRDO and other defence organisations.

(v) To publish scientific and technical journals including books and monographs of the DRDO.

Organisation of DESIDOC

Library: Known as Defence Science Library, it is the central reference library representing all major disciplines : of defence research and development. It has in its stock 1,32,300 volumes comprising books, reports, standards, specifications and bound periodicals. It receives 735 periodicals. It has a well—equipped section on Military Science and Engineering and maintains up-to-date collection of NASA and RAND reports. Besides providing library facilities to the local defence R and D Establishments, it arranges inter-library loan and supplies on demand, photocopies to outside defence R and D Establishments.

Documentation: The documentation activity comprises scanning, indexing, abstracting and further processing of information from current literature and dissemination in the form of the following current awareness services:

(i) DESIDOC – List of Current Scientific Literature (bimonthly)- This is an indexing service and contains Defence oriented R and D references, arranged subject-wise by Universal Decimal Classification.

(ii) SDI Bulletin (ad-hoc) – It is issued in sixteen series covering specific subject areas of defence R and D interest.

(iii) Patents Information Alerts (bimonthly) – This. is an abstracting service covering Indian and foreign patents. The service is supported by supply of copies of full patents on request.

(iv) Defence Reports Abstracts (bimonthly) – It gives abstracts of technical reports issued by NASA, NTIS, RAND (USA) and DRIC (UK) which are relevant to defence R and D projects.

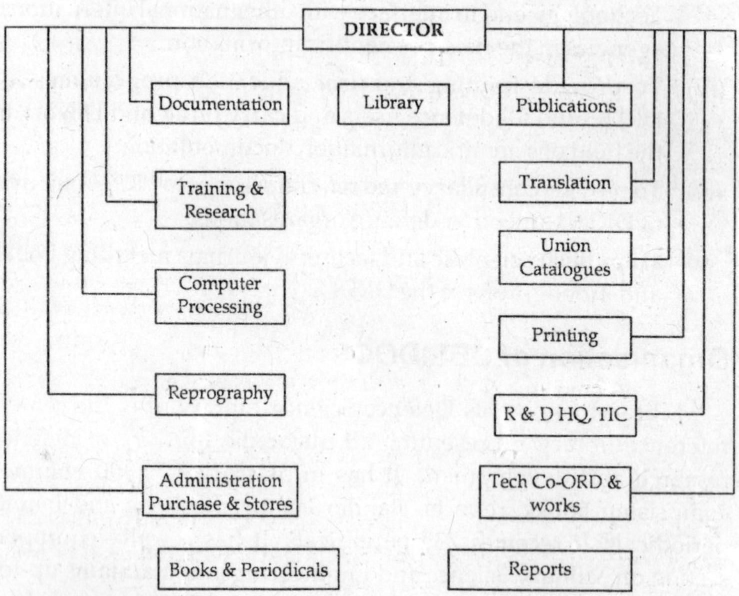

The SDI service at the moment is manually operated. It provides text in addition to the list of references, to users on the basis of their interest profile. The system is being computerised. Literature searches are conducted from primary and secondary sources for current as well as retrospective information and to bring out state of art/

literature survey reports on subjects of topical interest. A clipping service from central and regional newspapers is in operation which reports matters on DRDO, to the Scientific Adviser to Defence Minister and Chief Controllers of R and D.

GROWTH OF DEFENCE SCIENCE LIBRARY

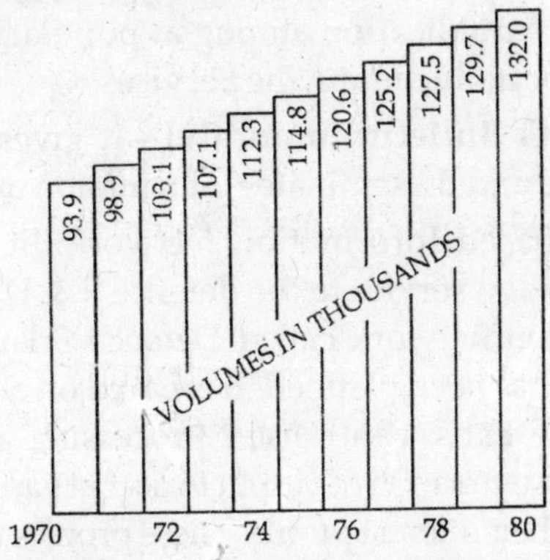

Translations: DESIDOC provides translation facilities for Russian, German, French and Japanese from its own resources. During the year 1980, about 2250 pages of foreign language material were translated into English. It also maintains a panel of external translators to cope up with the rising demand in these and other languages, for which manpower is not available in DESIDOC. It also issues 'Science Abstracts from Foreign Language Journals', a bimonthly bulletin, which has beer. found very useful by the users. Since 1980, a Translation Bank has been set up to collect translations available in defence R and D establishments and other civil institutions with a view to checking duplication in translation effort.

Publication: DESIDOC is responsible for disseminating the results of the research and development work carried out by defence R and D Estts. For this purpose it brings out R and D publications such as journals, brochures, proceedings of seminars/ conferences. The following journals are being issued:

(i) **Defence Science Journal (quarterly)**—It contains defence-oriented original research papers and review articles in various disciplines of science:

(ii) **R and D Digest (bimonthly)**—It gives the activities and attainments of defence R and D Labs/Estts and focuses attention on new developments taking place in other countries.

(iii) **R and D Bulletin (quarterly)**—It is a classified publication giving the achievements on R and D projects in DRDO.

(iv) **Popular Science and Technology (half yearly)**—This is an illustrative publication aiming at popularisation of defence science specially among the Services.

(v) **DESIDOG Bulletin (monthly)**—It gives the activities of DESIDOC and disseminates information of interest to TICS.

Computer-based Information Network: In order to provide efficient information service to the defence R & D Estts, a computer based information network called Defence Scientific Information System (DESIS) has been planned. It is based on decentralised input provided by the Estts, centralised processing at DESIDOC and decentralised dissemination of output to user at various Estts (through the Estts) as per their interest profile. These profiles will be continually updated on the basis of the feedback provided by them periodically. Besides input from the Estts, some relevant commercial data bases like NTIS, INSPEC, CAS, COMPENDEX will be subscribed to, in order to achieve wider coverage of the information sources. The system will provide project-oriented as well as mission-oriented information, in response to specific queries and also through SDI service.

Training: DESIDOC has launched an in-house training programme to provide adequate knowledge and skill to the officers and staff working in the Technical Information Centres of the defence R and D Labs/Estts, who do not possess formal professional training. The training courses on the following topics were held since 1980:

(i) **Indexing**—Three, courses, each of ten days' duration were held at Delhi, Hyderabad and Bangalore covering the defence R and D Estts located in and around these stations. These courses have been acclaimed highly useful by the participants as indicated in the feedback. Two more courses are planned at Pune and Delhi to cover the remaining DRDO Estts.

(ii) **Effective Technical Writing**—A ten days' course was held at Delhi in collaboration with the Central Institute of English and Foreign Languages, Hyderabad, to enable the scientists to present technical ideas in a clear and concise manner.

Union Catalogue Project: Towards effective resources sharing among defence R and D Estts, compilation of union catalogue has been started. Initially, the union catalogue of periodical holdings of the defence R and D Estts has been taken up. The data have been compiled on a standard format and will be finally computerised. In the subsequent phases, reports and books will be covered.

Supporting Services

Drawing and Design: The work involves preparation of technical drawings, illustrations and cover designs required for the DRDO publications. Varityping is also done for slidemaking and for preparing the matter for publications when these are to be printed by offset process.

Reprography: DESIDOC has a well-equipped section for xerography, microfilming, diazo printing, colour printing, photography and preparation of slides. Photographic projection, tape recording services are also provided for seminars/conferences.

Printing: Letter-press and offset facilities are available for carrying out the printing jobs of DESIDOC and of the defence R and D HQrs. The activity involves composing, block making, printing, duplicating and binding.

Technical Information Centre at Defence R and D HQrs

A Technical Information Centre has been set up in Sena Bhavan, New Delhi, to cater to the day-to-day requirements of the various offices located in the HQrs complex. It provides library and reprographic facilities.

Data Bases and Data Banks

Only well-organised information systems can cope up with constantly growing mass of information and effectively perform the process of communicating information. Computer techniques have found significant applications in the information field. Although, a computer can be used to perform almost all documentary functions, its main field of application lies in the retrieval and dissemination of information. This might be the reason for the emergence of computer-based information systems throughout the world. In India, the Department of Science and Technology (DST) has taken up the responsibility of developing a National Information System for Science and Technology (NISSAT). In this context, the computer facility already available at different institutions in the country is expected to be utilised for this purpose. In the three tier system, formulated in the NISSAT plan, specialized information systems in different specialties such as leather, aeronautics, food technology, drugs, electronics, etc., are envisaged with an integrated approach comprising facilities for exchange of information of all types with a network pattern. This necessitates creation of data bases for individual subject areas for the internally generated information and also use of commercially available data bases which are externally gene rated. An attempt is made in this paper to explain the data base concept as an important component of information system and some of the basic principles involved in its design and standardization.

Data Base Concept

History: During recent years, data base concept has been given greater attention by computer manufacturers, users, and academicians. In May 1969, a committee representing various groups held a series of meetings on data bases and presented its recommendations in a report entitled "A Survey of Generalized Data Base Management Systems"—this report is referred to as the CODASYL's first report. The major objective outlined in this report was the examination of the feasibility of implementing a common (generalized) data base system. Data definition, structure, levels of storage, management and programming facilities were examined with regard to generalized data base systems. In April 1971, the CODASYL Committee submitted a second report entitled, "Data Base Task Group (DBTG)" which updated the earlier report. The DBTG report highlighted the importance of implementing an independent data base.

Definition: The term data base has been defined in a number of ways in the computer science literature applying the terms only to on-line processing, calling all the files accessible to on-line system the data base and, apparently, leaving other files outside the base. Some authors define it as a collection of files brought together as a single file commonly accessible by a given set of programmes.

The CODASYL Committee used the terms data base, data bar and generalized data base synonymously to indicate the pool of interrelated data pertaining to an entity, tailored to achieve efficiency in creating, updating and retrieving data. According Rombergz. "In its most basic form, the data base consists of a of data elements, each of which is a unit of data that is complete in itself. These data elements are organized into logically related groups called data structures. Information files, are composed of a large number of data structures of the same type."

The difference between data base systems and conventional files can be seen at this point. The data files in a data base system are organized in a fashion that permits their use in several applications, rather than a single application.

Thus, in a data base system the focus shifts from a particular application and its specific input and output to a more general requirement for data files to serve a number of applications.

Bibliographical Data Base: Automated storage and retrieval has followed two main directions-bibliographic retrieval and data management. The data base concept discussed above was with reference to data management. Of course, the same could be used with advantage in bibliographical retrieval as well. In fact, research and development has gone into refining the techniques for indexing, abstracting, storing, retrieving and reporting of information from and about documents, as a result, large scale bibliographic data bases and retrieval services have been developed. Bibliographic data bases contain descriptive information about documents-books and periodical articles-the data typically included in these data bases are:

(a) document number;
(b) title;
(c) author;
(d) source reference;
(e) abstract;
(f) full text;
(g) indexing words or phrases;
(h) citations or number of references;
(i) organization from which the document is originating; and
(j) language in which the document is written.

Table 17.1. List showing Various Commercially Available Data Bases with Corresponding Printed Services

base	Printed version
DLARS	Index Medicus
INSPEC	Science Abstracts
C. A. SEARCH C. A. BIBLIO	Chemical Abstracts
SGI SEARCH	Science Citation Index
ERIC	Resources in Education
COMPENDEX	Engineering Index
METADEX	Metals Abstracts
BIOSIS	Biological Abstracts
Sociological Abstracts	Sociological Abstracts

Bibliographical data bases can broadly be divided into: (a) large discipline oriented data bases corresponding to a major abstracting journal such as Chemical Abstracts; (b) interdisciplinary data bases such as SCI SEARCH; (c) cross disciplinary data bases such as METADEX; (d) specialized data bases serving a particular technology such as RAPRA Abstracts; (e) data bases covering specific types of publications such as dissertation abstracts; and (f) data bases produced as a result of international co-operation. Examples of this type are INIS, AGRIS, etc.

Data Banks

The majority of machine-readable data bases, though formatted in a similar fashion to bibliographic data bases, store actual information rather than references. These are often referred to as data banks, and provide answers, facts and data in response to a query. The data banks store directory type of data pertaining to business, economics, social sciences, education and science and technology. FINTEL from Financial Times, DATA STREAM from Data Stream International Inc., and ISI SCITEL from Institute of Scientific Information could be cited as examples in this connection. A guide to data bases and data banks first published in 1975 and updated regularly ever since furnishes information regarding the growth in number of data bases and data banks. Table 2 indicates the figures for the period 1975 to 1978 pertaining to Europe.

Table 17.2. Growth of Data Bases and Data Banks in Europe

Year	1975	1976	1977	1978
No. of Data Bases	335	337	422	533
No. of Data Banks	51	149	268	568

Learned Information Directory (Ed. Alex Tomberg), published in 1980 covers 1,280 data bases and data banks presently available in U. S. A., Europe and other countries. Of these, 565 are bibliographic data bases and 715 are data banks. This only confirms the fact that data banks are on the increase compared to bibliographic data bases.

Data Base Design: As has been stated earlier, the data base concept is an advancement over the notion of an integrated set of files. The design of a data base will provide : tables of descriptions and interrelationships (structure) separate from the data (content) ; mechanisms for accessing the data elements and data sets directly or indirectly via indexes, pointers, conversion, computation; a capability for movement of individual data items or groups from the associations in which they are stored to the associations in which they are processed, and back to the storage ; protection of integrity and security of data items or groups of data items; management control of usage, content structure and optimization data that represent the activity of the enterprise.

Some General Principles: A necessary criterion in the creation of a data base - and one of its most essential characteristics – is that creators and users must agree on a common set of definitions for all the information in the data base. This is not so easy as it might seem. Elimination of data definitions in almost any medium to large scale user of data processing immediately exposes three classic problems: (1) synonymous, or identical items of data called by different names in different application environments ; (2) alternative definitions, or different systems using the same name to describe two different pieces of data; and (3) close definitions, or two different names used to describe different pieces of data with definitions so similar that there should be only one name and one definition.

Table 17.3. Subject Break-up of a Few Data Banks

Subject	No. of Data Balks
Aerospace	2
Agriculture	30
Armed Forces	1
Art, Literature, Music	1
Biology	6
Business and Economics	194
Chemistry	54
Civil Engineering	4
Demography and Geography	20
Earth and Space Sciences	21
Education	9
Electrical Engineering	11
Energy	13
Environment	32
History	1
Information and Documentation	1
Law	29
Linguistics	21
Mathematics	1
Mechanical Engineering	8
Medicine	48
Metals	10
Nucleonics	13
Paper, Printing Packages	7
Patents and Trade Marks	4
Petroleum	17
Physics	3
Social Sciences	8

Therefore, as a first step, the data base designers should develop a complete dictionary of definitions. After they obtain the support of the users for these definitions they must keep it current and enforce it fur new applications.

The next essential characteristic of significance in data base design and creation is deciding the data structure. Data structure has a bearing in the determination of processing the data and access procedures. There are two fundamentally different approaches to accessing the data. These are : sequential access organization and direct access. In sequential organization, records are located in sequence. This approach facilitates file maintenance but, requires extensive searching to locate individual records. On the other hand,' direct access permits the location of individual records' without searching, but is less efficient for maintaining a file with high activity. The storage media must be selected on the speed with which access to data is to be provided.

Bibliographic Record Format: The bibliographical data bases such as INSPEC, MEDLINE, CA SEARCH, COMPENDEX, etc., store information about documents, "such as books, periodical articles and technical reports, etc. The bibliographical description required to identify these documents is provided in varying degrees in each of these data bases.

The collection of information provided for a single document on machine-readable form as a self-contained unique logical structure, is often referred to as bibliographical record format. The purpose of such a format is to identify the document unambiguously and aid in its retrieval and also help the user in accessing its likely value in his search for pertinent information. Formal definitions for terms such as bibliographic description, bibliographic record, data elements, data fields, literature type and bibliographic level are provided in UNISIST Reference Manuals and are mostly accepted by the data base designers to a large extent.

The MARC Record format was originally designed by the Library of Congress and the British Library with the object of communicating bibliographic description in machine-readable form in such a way that records could be reformatted for any purpose. MARC – II superseded MARC. As more and more countries started using MARC, variations in. practice have made it deviate considerably from its original version. There are now several versions of MARC format, such as UK MARC, NRC MARC and so on.

The basic structure of UNIMARC complies with ISO 2709, the standard for bibliographic information interchange on' magnetic tape. The UNIMARC comprises two sections. Section, gives information describing the bibliographic data, while Section 2 holds the data itself. The segment of a magnetic tape pertaining to an individual record could graphically be represented as:

Record Label **Directory** **Control Fields** **Variable Fields**

Each record starts with a label and a directory, both of which are supplied by a programme. The label contains information about the record, such as, its length, and status (new record, changed record, etc.), type and class. The directory is a finding list, which provide$ for every tag, the tag, the number of characters in the field, and the starting character position within the record. In the MARC record, any element can be used as an access point.

Need for Standardization

In any computer-based information system, cost of producing data or information on machine-readable form constitutes a major portion of the cost involved in the project. It is only by sharing the data base among several user groups that cost effectiveness of the system could be achieved. This requires standardization in the design of data base to reduce confusion and increase compatibility. But, the question of establishing standards for use in exchange of material between various centres is not the same as trying to agree to universal system down to the last sub-field code. This is neither possible nor desirable. It is enough to freeze the machine-format which is the medium for exchange.

The most important factor to standardize is the structure (content format) of a data base. Ideally, the structure should be hospitable to all kinds of information, it should be independent of any particular hardware configuration, and should be uniform regardless of specific types of information it contains.

Formulation of standards for formats of fact files (data banks) is somewhat difficult task compared to bibliographic data bases. The format proposed by ISO-2709-1973 is suited to data bases designed to content-oriented search (data banks) techniques. In this context, tag-oriented structure is advocated for the data base design. Some national standard bodies such as British Standards Institution (BSI), American National Standards Institute (ANSI), ISO, etc., have developed standards covering : (a) Bibliographic Information Interchange Format for magnetic tape, (b) Magnetic Tape Labelling and File Structure for Information Interchange, and (c) Coded character sets for Information Interchange. All these could be used with considerable advantage in the design of machine-readable data bases. Apart from these, the UNISIST Reference Manual for Machine-Readable Bibliographic Descriptions will prove to be of immense value to any one intending to study about the bibliographic date bases. It may be stated that a clear distinction must be made by all data base designers between an internal format and an exchange format. The question of compatibility between these two types of formats will have to be studied carefully and a suitable solution be found out to achieve compatibility.

Conclusion

The advances in basic computer technology of cheaper storage, higher processing speeds, increased miniaturization of computer hardware and greater reliability associated with computer systems, made the use of these more attractive. The introduction of computer driven photo-composition machines and the availability of data base management techniques encouraged many of the producers of abstracting and indexing journals to adopt this technology in their journal production. As a result, machine-readable records of these products were obtained as an intermediary stage of their own journal production.

18

Automated Libraries

Introduction

The relationship between the library and the computer is a changing one. Computer science has been changing rapidly ever since its origins 20 years ago, and now the library itself is beginning to be changed under the influence of the machine. In a changing world, librarians have a responsibility not only to know about the ways in which libraries can use the techniques of automation, but also to be aware of the changes automation can bring to library service in the near and perhaps the more distant future.

It is easy in this twentieth century to strive for change simply for its own sake, just as it is even easier to strive for retaining the status quo. Those librarians whose task it is to decide for or against the particular change of automation need especially to be on their guard against these two attitudes. They need to make their decisions in the light of facts; facts about their Libraries as they are now; what services are provided to what people by what library staff and at what cost, and similar facts about any proposed system of Library automation; In this a library is no different from any other office or factory considering the use of a computer to perform a given job of work most economically. Where the difference does arise, however, is in the concept of a library's service. A factory may charge a certain price for its products and so, hopefully, make an overall profit on its operations. In such circumstances a computer can be shown to act either to increase or to reduce profits. But there are few libraries today which can be considered as existing in order to make a profit for their owners, or even required to balance an income from subscriptions against their expenses. How, then, can a price be set against the service which a library can provide, and how can this price be measured so that automation may be seen to be justified?

An answer to these questions can be found in two ways. Firstly, any industrial librarian knows that his job is to satisfy his company's information needs. He, a specialist in information work, can supply information to company employees more efficiently than they can obtain it themselves, and so the value of his library's service can be expressed in terms of minutes and hours of saved time, and hence in monetary terms. An analogous argument can be used of the reader service functions in university and public libraries. Secondly, the value of a library's service can also be expressed quantitatively in terms of the chief librarian's bargaining power at meetings of the library committee, and so in terms of the hard cash voted to him to enable him to run his library.

It is possible, therefore, although difficult, to express the value of automated library systems in quantitative terms and so to compare an automated library with its conventional counterpart. The decision to automate or not to automate can then be taken in the full light of the facts. That this decision seems frequently to have been taken in ignorance of the facts does not invalidate the argument, but serves merely to throw into clearer relief the well-known truths that librarians are, as a class, busy, that libraries struggle for enough money to buy all the books they want, let alone finance a proper automation feasibility study, and that it is much easier to obtain money to buy computer equipment than to buy books. Furthermore, once the computer is working in the library it is seldom difficult to show that improved standards of service have resulted, even though it has probably not been possible to reduce the staff' required, and even though the library's total overall expenditure will almost certainly' have risen.

The final situation then in most cases, will be that improved library service has been bought at a price. If the librarian has been able to justify this to his committee, then, according to my argument, the automated system has at least "broken even".

We must look a little more closely into the reasons why a librarian might consider using a computer in his library in order to improve its working in some way. And the first kind of reason, which we shall term emotional, is one unfortunate outcome of the automation revolution through which the advanced nations of the world are now passing. Because, according to the emotional argument, computers are modern and efficient, a library which uses a computer in some way must necessarily also be efficient and forward-looking, and almost certainly therefore a "good" library. It is indeed true to say that those libraries which have introduced computer systems are modern and forward looking. The automated systems may well be efficient and the library may be a good one. But it is certainly not necessarily true to say, as the emotional argument does, that if a library uses a computer then it will be all these things. That this reason exists at all, even if only as an attitude of mind, is a direct result of the false glamour ascribed to the computer and the shallow thinking and writing of those responsible for automating aspects of library routines. If, as seems likely, computers will fill a necessary role in libraries in the future, now is indeed the time for some libraries to experiment with ways and means of enabling computers to take their proper place in library work. These experiments should yield both qualitative and quantitative results. So far there have been too many of the former and too few of the latter kind.

Computerize Libraries

A computer is an electronic machine for manipulating symbols. For our purposes, we can readily make this definition more meaningful if we say that a computer can be regarded in many ways as being like a clerk. And if it is a clerk, then we may be able to use it to do clerical work in libraries more quickly, accurately, and more efficiently than it is done at present. It might even be possible to teach it some professional or intellectual jobs. Being a machine it should not tire under heavy work loads, and, in fact, should become more efficient as the work load increases so that as a library grows this can be accommodated without proportionate increases in staff.

From what we know about computer applications in other fields, we should expect automation to be feasible only in larger libraries or in cases where a number of smaller libraries combine together to form one large unit for processing purposes. However, we know also that computer time is growing steadily cheaper as newer, more advanced machines are developed, whereas the time of human clerks is becoming steadily more expensive. So we predict that automation will gradually became feasible in smaller libraries. This trend will be accentuated somewhat by the emergence of very small, cheap computers, but it must be remembered that many library applications require a large machine. The growth of on-line techniques, which are particularly suited to some areas of library work, will make it realistic for librariesto except to have on-line access to a large and powerful machine, rather than consider purchasing a small machine for their own use.

A well-established set of procedures exists, leading from the point we have now reached; that of having stated in general terms the advantages which might be expected to accrue from using a computer, to that of installing, testing; and running an automated system in a library. To follow all these procedures faithfully might seem pedantic, perhaps unnecessary in many circumstances, but it is necessary if the job is to be done honestly, avoiding emotion, cultivating reason, and working in quantitative terms. Because procedures will be enumerated and discussed in one particular way, it does not mean that this is the only way, or that different combinations and distributions of these procedures might not result in very different patterns of overall working; only that the basic ideas must follow one another in this way.

Measurement of Automated Libraries

The first step towards introducing an automated system is to carry out a feasibility study. This may be done at any level of detail, but the purpose is to ascertain whether or not a computer can be used to do a particular job more efficiently than heretofore. It can be an expensive stage, and may be broken down into two parts, the first one to ascertain if the feasibility study itself is worth undertaking. It is common knowledge that many such studies have shown that a computer was not really needed at all, and that the information gained from the feasibility study was sufficient to improve the existing system so as to make it more efficient than the automated one first contemplated.

It is during the feasibility study that systems analysis takes place. The system, be it the whole library itself or only one department, is analysed; its method of working is systematically taken apart piece by piece, so that in the end all the pieces are known and understood, as' are the ways in which they fit together to make the .whole. If only one department of the library is being investigated, the relationships between it and the other departments, and the library itself, must also be known and understood.

Measurement will also take place so that the final result of the study can be in quantitative terms. Numbers will be counted; the numbers of items bought, catalogued, lost, circulated, damaged, and the way these numbers may be expected to change in the future will be discovered. Also counted will be the number of people needed to do the various jobs in the system, and the time to do each job will be measured. It is very important that the end results of all this library activity be calculated or estimated. This can be difficult because it is not easy to apply a measure to a student reading a book, a chemist pleased with a morsel of information, or a housewife experimenting with new dishes described in a cookery book borrowed from her local public library. It must be attempted, however, because any automated system, as we have seen, is likely to alter the pattern of service offered by the library, and this is as important in the final evaluation as the numbers of books ordered each week, or the time it takes to discharge an overdue book.

From all these measurements the costs of the present system will be calculated. They will almost certainly be expressed as unit costs-the cost of cataloguing the "average" book, or answering the "typical" reference question. Together with details of the services performed by the present system and in particular any difficulties and problems associated with it, any aspects which are likely to become unsatisfactory in the light of future developments will be indicated, and all will be used by management to make an educated decision about the introduction of automation.

Because the introduction of computerized operations is not the only, and not necessarily the best solution to the problems that will have been brought to light, the next stage of the study is just to find the best solution, automated or not. It is highly desirable, therefore, that the study should be carried out by persons who have no direct interests in seeing that a computer system is installed, perhaps even using a particular make of computer. They should be perfectly free to advise on the optimal course of action. Likewise, the investigators should have considerable experience of similar studies, and be well informed on all data-processing and work-study techniques. Needless to say there is a great shortage of such people. Feasibility studies, therefore, are not cheap and so are often skimped or omitted entirely.

The end result of this second stage of the study is a broad system specification. It will indicate the hardware or machinery required and, in general terms, how everything will work. The throughput or work load handled will be given, as will the estimated costs. Staffing requirements will almost certainly be different from those of the old system, for keypunchers will replace clerks (a clerk can be trained to keypunch, of course) and it will be necessary to have a senior staff member, with data-processing experience, in charge of operations and one or two programmers may be required on a permanent basis. Staff requirements will be very different where a library installs a computer for its own use, from the case where it merely uses a short time each week or someone else's machine.

Manual and Automated Libraries

Computers work in ways radically different from human beings, the flow of work in an automated system can differ quite considerably from that in the corresponding manual system. Old departmental barriers can therefore be broken down on the introduction of automation, as similar processes in different departments are combined and as duplication of work is eliminated. The overall organizational structures of the library can be materially altered, and this will be appreciated and stated in the feasibility study.

Once an automated system is considered in any detail it is apparent that it offers a range of possible products and services considerably wider than does a conventional system. The compilation of all kinds of statistics is but one example of this. A library can expect, therefore, to expand the scope of its operations by introducing mechanized routines, and it is desirable either that the team doing the study include a good knowledge of library service among their skills, or that one member of the library staff work closely with the team, in order that the full possibilities of wider operations are realized.

From the final report of the feasibility study it should be a comparatively simple matter for the library management to decide on a course of action. Only in the largest libraries would a feasibility study be likely to indicate clear overall cost reductions through introducing automated methods. In other libraries the situation would almost certainly be that at the present time a computer-aided system would cost more but would bring additional advantages. It is up to the management to decide whether these advantages justify the increased costs, bearing in mind that, in time, costs will tend to change in favour of automation.

If we assume that a decision is made in favour of automation, where does the library go from here? The answer is that the next stages in this idealized introduction of mechanization will depend very considerably on the extent of the automation which is planned, on the organizational framework of which the library is a part, and on what we can term the library's computing environment.

The procedures for implementing an automated circulation system, for example, will be different from those required by a system embracing all a library's technical processing routines. In a university environment the library would expect to make use of a central university computing facility rather than purchase its own machine or use the services of a commercial bureau. This will affect not only the type of machine used, which is likely to be better suited to mathematical than to library work, and the languages programs are written in, but also, because programming may well be done in the computing laboratory, it will affect the staffing requirements in the library. The overall computing policy of the organization of which any library is a part will also affect such factors as, for example, the frequency with which computer runs can be made, or whether on-line working is, or is planned to be, available, and so be an important factor in the design of the library system. In large organizations it not infrequently happens that a library in another division or department has already automated some of its functions. It may be possible to take these programs over just as they stand or with only small modifications.

It is quite possible for one person, or one group of persons, to carry out both of these two steps, in which case the distinction between them is obscured. Alternatively, the second step, which has more of the character of straightforward routine than the first, can be performed by a programmer. In either case it is absolutely vital that at the stage of system design proper (step one) all the implications for the library of the various detailed decisions and operations which will be included in the final program are fully understood. This requirement can be achieved, as during the feasibility study, by having a senior library staff member work with the system design group, but, ideally, the system designer or designers should themselves be experienced librarians. Similarly, it is best for the programming to be done by someone with a good knowledge of librarianship. Here, however, we come face to face with some very real problems associated with the fact, mentioned at the very beginning of this chapter, that this whole subject of automation in libraries is a relationship between two disciplines.

Few people, even nowadays when their great worth is appreciated, are at the same time experienced librarians and knowledgeable and up to date in computing matters. If it is vital that an automated library system be designed with all its implications for librarianship in mind, it is, at the very least, highly desirable that the programs are written so as to make the system as efficient as possible from a computing point of view. So library systems are very often designed as a co-operative venture between library and computing department staff in order to assemble together the necessary skills and expertise. The work is often done as a sideline, or even in staffs' own time. That so much sound work has been done on this basis is a tribute to those involved, but progress could have been more rapid and more quantitative analyses made had these methods of working been less common. Where it is difficult to find the time to design and implement an automated system, the detailed analyses and comparisons necessary for its full justification and evaluation naturally tend to be skimped of omitted. Overall impressions are substituted and, as a result, the library profession is all the poorer. And not only this, but an atmosphere is cultivated wherein the arguments of emotion can flourish.

Programming Language for Software

The languages in which computer programs for library routines are written are important subjects for discussion at the present time. For mathematical, commercial, and other special kinds of work, a umber of high-level programming languages have been defined.

These make it easy for the programmer because the programming language can be quite similar in form and content to the language ordinarily used in the particular discipline. The price paid for this programming facility is a less efficient use of machine time. This is important in one-off jobs, but it becomes a major factor in library systems where a program is run frequently. A further advantage of high-level language is that they can often be run on many different makes and types of computer; on all machines, in fact, for which a special translating or compiler program has been written. This takes each instruction in the high-level language and converts it into the necessary number of detailed machine instructions for the computer concerned. Programs written in high-level languages can thus be exchanged widely, to the overall conservation of programming manpower.

Because of the machine inefficiency of high-level languages, library programs tend to be written in what are termed low-level languages. These make better use of computer time but, being less similar to natural language and requiring the use of quite detailed instructions, make greater demands on the programmer's time and ability. They are generally applicable to only one make or series of computers, and so do not permit free exchange and utilization of programs. In a situation where computing power is at a premium, library programs will tend to be written in low-level languages at the expense of programming manpower. Where programming manpower is at a premium, the tendency will be to use high-level languages at the expense of computing power. Present trends are beginning to indicate that, in future, library programs will be written in high-level languages and exchanged freely in order to save the very considerable effort which would be entailed were each library to design and program its own systems. Should a language specially suited to library work ever be written, then this would enable these programs to be less wasteful of machine time.

When a program has finally been written, it must then be tested, or "de-bugged", to remove as many as possible of the errors which the fallible human system-designers and programmers will have written into it. This is generally done by running the program with test data to simulate as many as possible of the circumstances that are likely to arise in real-life working. It is at this stage that the value of an experienced programmer is most apparent. He will have written fewer errors into the program to start with and will be able to discover more readily why things go wrong when they do, and be able to put them right. Programming skill in this respect is particularly valuable when working with low-level languages.

After this stage the program is ready to begin work with real library data, but it is usual to place one more safeguard against error in the machine system by working the new system in parallel with the old for a few months. After this period, if everything is satisfactory, the support provided by the old system in event of failure of the new is removed and the automated system, having been thoroughly tried, takes over full responsibility. Machines, of course, like human beings, are not infallible and they do from time to time make mistakes or break down. A "safety net" must therefore be provided so that in the event of machine failure no data is lost and the system can carry on, or safely suspend operations until the failure can be rectified. Such a safety net can be provided with a coarse or with a fine mesh, the latter being more expensive.

Implementation of Software in Library

Once an automated library system is working satisfactorily, it becomes important that it should continue to do so. Procedures in the event of machine failure are only one aspect of this general problem. Equally important is the need to establish a good working relationship between the library and the computing department so that the desired standard bf library service is maintained. A library system usually demands that a computer run be made at a stated time each day, week, or month. For example, where a university library has introduced a computerized circulation system, it is necessary that an updated printout of books on loan should be available in the circulation department each day. If anything causes this printout to be delayed, then the work of the circulation department will be hindered. In fact, in the case of circulation control it is true to say that the whole justification of an automated system hinges on the daily printout being available at the right time each day.

Library work must often therefore receive high priority in the, computing department, and this can be difficult to achieve. In some organizations, however, computing policy, and thus the order of priority of the different users, is determined by a special computing committee and not by the head of the computing department. If the library can put a sufficiently strong case to such a committee, then the necessary degree of priority will be guaranteed and, consequently, the desired quality of library service ensured. In some instances the first move towards library automation comes from within the computing department, and then this difficulty should not arise if the importance of priorities is emphasized by the librarian from the early stages of the project.

The implications for libraries of this state of flux are very considerable, especially since, until recently, libraries have exhibited only a very slow rate of change. Librarians, despite or perhaps because of the conservatism they display in relation to changes in libraries, show a remarkable interest in the very latest computing techniques that are either still in the early experimental stages or no more than ideas in designers' brains. These future developments invariably hold out the promise of solving all the world's problems of bibliographic organization, and, perhaps not unnaturally, librarians grasp eagerly at them. But when the full implications of such developments are pointed out in terms of the sacrifices and changes each library would have to make in order to adopt them, then the former panacea can become less attractive.

Once a program has been implemented in a library it will not be long before the need will become apparent to make small additions and changes to it. These must be done by a programmer and will sometimes involve considerable alterations in the whole structure of the program. Where automation in a library has progressed beyond an elementary stage, it will become very desirable for the library to have a programmer on its permanent staff' and perhaps a more senior person, a systems analyst, as well. A embryonic data-processing department will have been created within the library because of this requirement for constant minor change and improvement. It will have responsibilities in all the conventional library departments where automated routines have been introduced and must have the authority to see that any changes are made in such a way that they satisfy the requirements of efficiency laid down for the system itself.

Once such a department of data processing has been established, a library will be in a good position to keep abreast of advances in computer science and will be able to modify the library's own systems from time to time to take fullest advantage of changes in the facilities offered in the computing unit where the library's work is done. Being actually on the library's own permanent staff, members of the library data-processing department will be able to take full account of the librarianship aspects of their work. This is the ideal situation, and where a library is introducing automation on anything more than a very limited scale, the establishment of such a department should be given high priority.

In order to complete this picture of libraries and automation it is necessary to try to look a short distance into the future, to see what developments are likely to come about in computing and how libraries will be able to use them. Because of the rapid rate of change in the field of automation, such future knowledge becomes essential if one is fully to understand the present situation and to know how to plan for library systems which will become operational in a few years' time.

Future of Software

There is one fairly recent development in this field which should be of the greatest importance in the future. And because here is something which is with us now, holding potentially great possibilities for the future, it is possible to speak with some certainty. There now exist in . Britain a number of working parties, each active in some areas of the field of library automation. Each owes its existence to the fact that a number of libraries are co-operating and pooling their resources to speed progress. Some of the working parties are designing systems for a particular make of computer, while others have no such limitation. Some are concentrating on the problems of one particular type of library, while others consider all types of library. It is beginning to seem likely that when these groups finally produce viable systems each will be adopted with little or no change by several libraries. One group in particular is designing a book-ordering system in such a way that it includes most of the features required by libraries and can readily be altered to cater for special individual preferences. Programs will be written in COBOL so that they will not be limited to one make or model of computer.

This co-operation will be of the greatest importance in future. Now, and always, it makes possible savings in programming effort and speeds the introduction of automation where this has been shown to be justified. When cataloguing data in machineable form becomes more generally available, for example, its use by individual libraries will be facilitated where numbers of libraries are using identical or similar cataloguing systems. The situation will be similar where a new technique or piece of equipment becomes available to a group of libraries which are using one type of computer. A new improved program need be written once only to be capable of adoption by all members of the group. Once a group of libraries have automated all or some of their activities and have proved this to be an advantage, other libraries will find it to their advantage either to adopt the common systems as they stand or with the minimum possible alterations. Among university libraries at least, programs will be made available freely.

It is much easier to talk of library co-operation in this way than to achieve it in practice. Although all libraries are the same to the extent that they buy, catalogue, store, and lend books and other material they do differ considerably in that they buy different kinds of books catalogue them in different ways, and serve many different types of readers. Accordingly, libraries have developed in many different ways and rightly so. But it is nonetheless true that when comparing the various methods of performing a given job, the differences tend to be in matters of detail, and that underneath is a large area of common practice. This makes it reasonable to expect that co-operating libraries will be able to accept large segments of automated systems as they stand and will need to alter only details. It is true that some apparently trivial differences in points of detail can make the adoption of a whole system impossible, but such cases are the exception rather than the rule.

(a) Small libraries, having simple cataloguing needs and buying straightforward material from a limited number of suppliers.

(b) Medium and large libraries, buying a wide range of materials from all parts of the world, with cataloguing needs more complex than type (a) but not so demanding as (c) Full control of circulation is needed and individual treatment, particularly as regards cataloguing, is required for special collections. Most university and public libraries would fall into this class.

(c) National and other very large libraries with complex acquisition procedures for all types of library materials. Fully detailed cataloguing is necessary for very large catalogues which may have to be related to the production of a national bibliography.

This tendency towards standardization is, of course, to be observed in most aspects of life today. Its advantage is to be found in the reduction of costs it makes possible. Despite our understandable attachment to our differences, we accept standardization because of the clear advantages it offers. A good illustration for our purposes can be seen in the motor industry. People's transport needs tend to fall into a small number of well-defined classes, and so do the types of motor-car that are produced. A fair amount of individual differences in needs and preferences are catered for by different manufacturers and by the addition of optional extras to basic designs. And so with libraries. Very many individual needs and preferences can be catered for by adding "optional extras" to the above three design types, and further variety will be ensured by the fact that differing systems will be produced by the various working parties mentioned above.

Included in this concept of standardization of library systems is greater uniformity in cataloguing practice and subject identification. A small number of universal schemes for classification and subject indexing will be adopted by more and more libraries. These universal schemes are with us already and, despite their acknowledged short-comings, libraries have already begun to change over to using them. The advantages to be gained from uniformity and the resulting ability to buy usable cataloguing copy from a central source are considered to make worthwhile the very great task of conversion involved, for example, in reclassifying a library's whole collection.

Automated Cataloguing

The greatest pressures towards standardization will come in this urea of cataloguing as a result of advances in the practice of librarianship that are associated with the introduction of automation. Three events are combining together at the present time which are potentially Capable of effecting very great changes in library practice throughout the world. Firstly, the Library of Congress Shared

Cataloging Program is extending the scope of the Library of Congress printed catalogue card service to include all material from western European countries. Secondly, the introduction of standard book numbering in Britain, besides facilitating the acquisition of books by libraries, provides a unique tag for each book which can readily be handled by computer, and enables cataloguing copy for new books to be recorded by the C British National Bibliography from 3 to 6 weeks before publication. If standard book numbering is adopted by other countries, and there is good reason to hope that it will be, then the cataloguing copy provided by the Library of Congress shared Cataloging Program will also be available a similar period before publication. The third event, or rather programme of events, is the Library of Congress MARL (MachineReadable Cataloging) Project. When this has been fully implemented it will make the cataloguing copy, collected in advance of publication by the Shared Cataloging Program, available to libraries in machineable form. The format of these machineable catalogue records is designed to facilitate the exchange of cataloguing copy between libraries and to enable individual libraries to modify and adapt the records to their own particular needs.

Such modification can be of two kinds, programmable and non programmable. Programmable alterations can be performed automatically by the computer when the machineable catalogue record is added to the library's own internal records. They include standard abbreviating operations on headings, descriptions, and classification numbers, and the reformatting of entries. The basic idea behind such programmable alterations is that they are standard. Non-programmable alterations involve human intervention and are needed whenever part of a catalogue record must be changed to some form that cannot be derived by algorithm from the original record. All such alterations cost money and the non-programmable ones will be the more expensive of the two kinds.

Centrally produced cataloguing copy, of course, has been with us for some time, and it has been bought by many libraries, especially in the United States. Two drawbacks have prevented its more widespread use; the comparative slowness of the services and the low percentage of libraries' total acquisitions covered. Both these disadvantages should soon be overcome and, in regard to the second, large libraries should expect to have approximately 70-80 per cent of their new acquisitions covered by the Library of Congress service. Librarians have long realized the advantages of central cataloguing services and have been aware of the great waste of effort when books are catalogued in each library where copies are bought. Now, it is likely that this longstanding dream will soon materialize.

Union Cataloguing

Another librarians' dream may also be realized over the next few 'decades as a result of this co-operation in cataloguing: the national machineable union catalogue. This idea of a national catalogue giving the holdings of all libraries in the country and also containing entries for all new books as they are published, able to be searched by computer from remote on-line terminals, appears to librarians to solve very many of the problems that they have today. There are very great obstacles to be overcome before such a catalogue can be made a reality, but work being done now leads one to expect that it will eventually come to exist. Machineable copy for all new books is almost with us and the investigations now in progress on how to convert the entries in the British Museum catalogue to machineable form should enable a very large corpus of existing catalogue material to be included in the national catalogue. The very real difficulties in programming a machine catalogue search by author and title, caused by inconsistencies in cataloguing, can be overcome by standard book numbers for new books and for old ones. Direct access. computer memories are rapidly increasing in size and should cause no serious problems. The remote on-line techniques are already with us.

The advantages of such a catalogue are considerable. Primarily, it will give the locations of material listed in it and remove almost all the inefficiency and frustration from existing systems of inter-library lending. As such, it will be a major adjunct to national scholarship. Libraries will be able to extract cataloguing data for new acquisitions directly from it by means of on-line consoles. This act will automatically indicate a location in that library for the items concerned. Local catalogues, whether printed on paper or kept only in machine memory, will list the most frequently used material only. Thus, great savings will be realized in catalogue printing costs or in machine memory storage devoted permanently to library catalogues. Uniformity in cataloguing practice will be further encouraged. It is questionable, however, whether such a catalogue will be searchable by subject.

From this point on, librarians' dreams of the future begin to bring the handling of textual material within the scope of systems of automation. Facsimile transmission of photographs is an everyday occurrence in the newspaper industry where speed is all important and where the volume of information is comparatively small. Transmission of printed pages by these means is practicable and economical over short distances where there is a high traffic density, but up to the present there has been little demand from libraries for higher transmission speeds than those provided by sending photocopies through the post.

Prophecies of libraries where the codex and the printed page have been :replaced by digital storage devices and where a computing facility has taken over the task of literature searching is very exciting and attractive, both to librarians and to those scholars who really are overwhelmed by their century's information explosion. Although many people would regret the passing of the codex and although the combination of the printed page, the codex, and the library is embarrassingly efficient as a machine for storing data and providing rapid random access to it, there is no doubt that many research workers would welcome real assistance with their information gathering problems.

19

Information Retrieval in Automated Library

An IBM 370/155 system at the Indian Institute of Technology, Madras, is being used, among other things, for implementing the CAN/SDI experimental project, for operating the police information system for the Tamil Nadu Government, and for developing other management information systems.

The Tata Institute of Fundamental Research, Bombay, is equipped with a CDC 3600 system with support facilities. Recently, a DEC 1077 system with a PDP 11 support was also installed.

An augmented IBM 360/44 system at the Indian Institute of Science, Bangalore, is being used for studies in computer science, information processing and automation, computer searching of chemical substructures, image processing and linguistics.

The computer facilities at Delhi University and the Indian Statistical Institute, Calcutta, are respectively being used by INSDOC and DRTC for research and development in information storage and retrieval. The ICL 1903 computer ;at the Hindustan Machine Tools Limited, Bangalore, the IBM 1401 and IBM 7044 computers at the Indian Institute, Kanpur, and the IBM 1620 system at the Central Mechanical Engineering Research Ins'titute (CMERI), Durgapur, are some of the computer installations that are also suited for library automation and information retrieval applications.

Several industrial organizations as well as some central and state government agencies such as the Office of the Registrar General (Census Operations); the Central Statistical Organization, and the Life Insurance Corporation of India, have been using computers for data processing and information storage and retrieval. More recently, electronic computers are being put to an increasing variety of applications in India. These include:

- Patent data monitoring and cardiological studies in hospitals and medical research institutions.
- Police information systems.
- Chemical structure coding and searching.
- Online seismic data processing.
- Climatological data processing.
- Image processing.

Computerization of information retrieval involves large amounts of data input, relatively few possessing operations, and a fairly large amount of output, in contrast to computational applications in scientific and technical research and development which involve low volume input/ output operations and large volume of processing operations. Manipulation of large data files and fast access to large volumes of data call for large and inexpensive computer memories and fast input/ output devices. A combination of magnetic tape and disk memories is necessary Tapes provide inexpensive large-volume memory, and disks provide fast, random access to data.

Applications of Computers

Application of computers to library and information work will be discussed under the following two general headings:

(1) Library Automation: This includes the use of computers to aid in the house-keeping operations in libraries, such as acquisition, serials control, circulation controls cataloguing, and union catalogue production.

(2) Information Retrieval: This includes the use of computers. for generating index entries for the storage and selective retrieval of bibliographic data for such applications as. reference service, compiling bibliographies, and selective dissemination of information.

AUTOMATED LIBRARY

Need & Purpose

Many university libraries and special libraries in India are large enough to computerize at least some of their house-keeping operations, and many of these libraries operate within environments where computer facilities already exist. Those libraries that have attempted computerization have approached the project in a pioneering spirit because of the relatively recent introduction of computers to other applications. The advantages and problems of computerization in the library have been actively debated upon by librarians and information system specialists. Such discussions are largely based on the experience of American and European libraries reported in literature. Most of the projects are small scale efforts of an experimental nature, designed to study the technical feasibility, economic viability and operational considerations. All the projects have attempted to computerize one or a few house-keeping operations rather than all the operations of a given library unit. For example, L.J. Haravu's experimental project on the computerized acquisition of serials concentrated on the generation and periodical updating of a master serials file, and production of various lists periodically for serials control ; it did not include, for example, the checking-in of serials.

(1) To investigate the technical and operational feasibility of computerized library routines.

(2) To expedite the production of union catalogues, indexes and other similar information retrieval and professional. tools.

(3) To streamline operational procedures and achieve uniformity in the quality of products such as the union catalogue.

(4) To benefit from the computer facilities already available within the environment in which the library is opening.

(5) To achieve some savings in costs.

Savings in man-power does not seem to be a dominant consideration.

Acquisition

In the acquisition department operated manually, the items selected for acquisition are first recorded on cards or slips of paper, and this file is re-arranged manually in several sequencers, e.g. alphabetically by author or title to check with the card catalogue, or alphanumerically by order number to receive and incorporate status reports from book-sellers and publishers until the books are received. Manual arrangement of files and creation of multiple copies of records for maintaining various files are tedious and time-consuming processes, and are prone to errors. In the computerized acquisition department, once the basic record is created on a machine-readable medium, the file of such records can be easily manipulated, and a variety of lists can be generated periodically or upon demand for keeping track of orders and expenditure.

Serials Control

The nature of serials (multi-component publications arriving in parts over a long period of time), (2) the complexties of the acquisition process necessitating continuous monitoring of the serial issues for which prepayment has been made, and claiming the parts that fail to arrive, (3) difficulties involved in dealing with a number of groups of people such as publishers, jobbers and binders whose motivations and methodologies are often divergent, (4) the need for maintaining an elaborate recording system to monitor receipt of current issues and display retrospective holdings, and (5) the need for continuous budgetary control to monitor allocation, encumbrances and expenditures under a multiplicity of headings. Computerization of serials control can greatly facilitate some or all of the above tasks ranging from acquisition, checking-in of current issues, generation of claim notices and a variety of records and listings including serials routing slips and binding records.

(1) Alphabetically by title;
(2) subject lists (by UDC class number);
(3) country of publication;
(4) publisher;
(5) frequency;
(6) vendor; and
(7) mode of acquisition (i.e. subscription, gift, exchanger or membership).

Objective of Serial Control

(1) Production of renewal lists;

(2) sending of overdue claims;
(3) production of fortnightly list of periodicals received in the library;
(4) production of binding lists of periodicals received in full and ready for binding; and
(5) alerting of special cases (e.g. when a periodical has not been received at all or when there are too many gaps in the receipt of a periodical).

At the CMERI, Durgapur, a computer program has been developed for its IBM 1620 computer to simplify the routines of storage, retrieval and updating of serials information. The system can handle 2,000 serials, and can be expanded to accommodate 10,000 serials The library attached to the Physical Research Laboratory, Ahmedabad, has also contemplated the development of a computerized acquisition routine for serials.

Circulation Control through Computer

The circulation section has to maintain files that can provide the following information

(1) Information about a given book : To whom issued and when it is due.
(2) Information about a given borrower : What books are issued and when they are due.
(3) Information about overdue books.
(4) Information on books placed on reserve by borrowers.

Computerised Cataloguing

Computerized cataloguing is feasible if cataloguing can be made a centralized and shared effort at a regional or national level. The MARC (Machine Readable Cataloguing) project of the United States Library of Congress, and more recently, the Ohio College Library Center (OCLC) project, are outstanding examples of the successful computerization of centralized and shared cataloguing currently operational in the United States of America. It should be remembered that in computerized cataloguing, the intellectual process of subject analysis, classifying, and creation of the original catalogue entry should still he done by human cataloguers. The computer can take over the clerical tasks of creating multiple entries from the basic catalogue entry, editing, alphabetizing and merging of entries, and the physical production and duplication of the catalogue in card or book format. It is therefore more appropriate to talk about computer-aided cataloguing rather than computerized cataloguing. Other possible advantages of computer-aided cataloguing include frequent generation of accession lists, creation of a national bibliography, preparation of author and subject bibliographies, centralized distribution of catalogue cards, savings in original cataloguing effort in participating libraries, and possibly, selective dissemination of information (SDI) and online bibliographical information retrieval. There does not appear to be any definitive move in the direction of computer-aided cataloguing in India.

Computerised Union Catalogue

The earliest attempt to mechanize union catalogue production in India was reported in 1963 by Saha and Halder of the Indian Statistical Institute, Calcutta. This project used unit record equipment.

The union catalogue project itself was initiated in INSDOC in 1959; but the first attempt to use a digital computer to produce the union catalogue was made in a project conducted at the Indian Institute of Technology; Kanpur, in 1964. The object of this project was not only to assess the extent to which the computer could be used to process the union catalogue, but also to gain some definitive impressions on the prospects and problems of using the digital computer far processing non-arithmetical data and the possibility of using the computer in other routines of INSDOC. One hundred entries from INSDOC's union catalogue were converted into machine-readable form and a master file was created. Programmes were written to manipulate the master file to alphabetize the entries, and to produce alphabetic, geographic and chronological indexes, using the IBM 1620 computer.

This pioneering experimental project was followed up by a larger project for compiling a union catalogue of scientific and technical periodicals available in some 89 libraries in Mysore State (now Karnataka State) since 1965.

The Regional Union Catalogue of Scientific Serials: Bombay-Poona, containing information on about 8,000 serials in 66 libraries was produced by INSDOC in 1973 using the IBM System/360 Model

44 computer available at the Delhi University Computer Center. This was the thirteenth number in the union catalogue series of INSDOC.

COMPUTERIZED INFORMATION RETRIEVAL

Overview

Although application of computers to library procedures in India has been somewhat slow and sporadic, the development of computerized information storage and retrieval systems has been going on quite vigorously in a few institutions of research and higher education. A major impetus to the development of computerized information storage and retrieval systems was given by S.R. Ranganathan in 1967. He outlined the fundamental components and operations of a computerized document retrieval system in which the basic operations include the classification of subjects of documents and questions according to a freely-faceted classification scheme:

(1) synthesize the class number for the subjects of both documents and queries from kernel terms derived by facet analysis;

(2) search, select and display, in desired format, details of documents relevant to the query; and

(3) generate class index entries on the basis of chain procedure to provide an alphabetical approach to the subjects of documents.

Ranganathan a cautioned against excessive dependence on the computer and the naivette that the application of computer would solve all the problems of librarians and information scientists. The facet analysis of the subjects of documents and queries – which is fundamental to the successful design and implementation of the DOC-FINDER system, is very much an intellectual operation to be performed by human analysts. The computer is an electronic tool that has to be used judiciously to expedite the repetitive, non-intellectual processes and to handle large volumes of data. Subsequent developments in computerized information retrieval in India have been largely inspired and influenced by this philosophy.

The major thrust of developments in India has been along three well-defined lines : (1) Computer-assisted indexing, (2) developing a computer-based document retrieval system, and (3) selective dissemination of information as an ongoing activity for current awareness. Although these may appear to be independent directions of development, it is easy to see that the successful implementation of a selective dissemination of information program presupposes the existence of a computerized document finding system which, in turn, is dependent on the development of a computerized document surrogation system.

Subject Indexing

The subject indexing of documents for providing a subject approach is essentially an intellectual task. However, certain phases of indexing such as generation of cross-references and display of index entries, are amenable to computerization. A. Neelameghan has shown that a theory-based classification scheme – one in which classifying the subjects of documents is based on the use of postulates, canons and principles of the general theory of classification – can lend itself to computer-simulation. A freely-faceted analytico-synthetic classification scheme facilitates computer simulation of the assembly of components of a subject, resulting in a class number or a structured subject reading coextensively representing the given subject. The main steps in classifying the subjects of documents are:

(1) Determining the kernel ideas forming components of the subject;
(2) determining the inter-relation and mutual filiation among the component kernel ideas, by the principles of facet analysis;
(3) arranging the component ideas in the sequence of their mutual filiation; and
(4) representing the subject in the form of (a) a string of terms and/or (b) a class number consisting of a string of digits in a preferred notational system.

POPSI

The first step, viz., selection of kernel ideas, is essentially an intellectual process, and has to be performed by the classifier by studying the document. This step is not readily amenable to computerization. The remaining three steps can be computer-simulated by using either the schedules of the classification scheme or a specially constructed alphabetical index to the classification schedules.

Research work on the computerization of subject indexing at DRTC is largely based on the above considerations. "Postulate-based Permuted Subject Indexing" (POPSI) is an indexing procedure for deriving subject headings and subject index entries. Computer programs for generating POPSI subject index entries were written in COBOL language for the ICL 1901 A computer. Computer programs have also been developed at DRTC for generating a KWAC (Keyword And Context) index and for chain indexing ; these programs are in PLAN-3 language for use on ICL 1900 series computers. Some work on thesaurus construction has also been reported.

Since 1967, INSDOC has been compiling a computer-aided keyword subject and author index to Indian Science Abstracts. The index entries assigned by indexers are punched onto IBM punch cards and processed through an IBM 1620 computer. The processing consists of alphabetizing and editing the index entries, and printing them in 70-character index lines. The monthly indexes are cumulated to produce an annual index. The main advantages of using the computer are Elimination of the tedium of manual alphabetization of the index entries, improved accuracy by reducing typographical errors, and faster production of the indexes. With the aid of the computer, it takes less than six days to prepare the final press copy of the monthly index, and costs about Rs. 400 per issue. The annual cumulated index takes less than six hours of computer time, and costs about Rs. 1,500.

In another indexing project, INSDOC collaborated with the Indian Standards Institution in the production of a subject index to the annual Handbook of ISI Publications. The basic format and procedures were similar to those of the keyword index to Indian Science Abstracts described above. Absence of lower case letters and Greek characters, and lack of see and see also cross-references were some of the problems encountered in these projects. Additional problems such as the lack of facility for printing subscripts and superscripts in chemical notation were experienced in another experimental project to produce a computerized KWOC (keyword out of context) index to the Indian Journal of Technology. The programs for this project were written in the SPS-IID language for the IBM 1620 computer.

Document Retrieval

One of the earliest studies on the use of a general purpose digital computer for information storage and retrieval was an experimental project carried out at INSDOC during 1966. The main objective of this project was to gain experience in (a) storing data on disk, (b) retrieving data in response to specific queries, and (c) printing out lists of data retrieved. The retrieval program covered four types of search strategies : (1) Single-aspect search ; (2) logical product search; (3) between-the-limits search ; and (4) search for upper limit of an item of data. The IAEA's Directory of Nuclear Reactors, volume 1: Power Reactors, was used as the data source for this experiment. Programs were written in FORTRAN and were run on an IBM 1620 computer.

(1) The input consists of document entries classified by a freely-faceted analytico-synthetic classification scheme.

(2) The class number of the subject of each document could be automatically synthesized from the kernel terms of the subject, and

(3) The computer could synthesize an appropriate class number for a query from the kernel terms of the facet analyzed subject of the query, and select document entries appropriate to the query.

The system would also facilitate title and author searches and provide for browsing of the output entries by the reader. The database (called Catalogue-on-Tape) of the document finding system consists of a classified part and an alphabetical part.

As a part of this project, a program package consisting of fifteen computer programs written in Autocoder language for the general purpose digital computer IBM 1401. These programs can also be used on other computers such as those of the IBM 1400 series and 7000 series, provided suitable intermediate conversion languages are available. Some programs were also written in PLAN language for the ICL 1900 series computers.

Features

(1) Retrospective search for entries relevant to a query on the basis of subject, author, collaborator, series, etc.

(2) SDI service based on user interest profile expressed in terms of class numbers or feature headings.

(3) Assembly of the components of class number for the subject of a document or of a query using the classification schedules stored on tape.

(4) Translation of class number into kernel terms to form a structured feature heading.

(5) Generation of alphabetical indexes of various kinds, e.g. KWIC, KWOC and POPSI on the basis of feature headings.

(6) Generation of output in different formats of the main entry.

(7) Output on line printer, punched card or magnetic tape.

(8) Updating the Catalogue-On-Tape database, readers profiles and classification schedules on tape.

(9) Interactive question negotiation and searching in which the reader receives computer assistance in selecting appropriate terms for query formulation.

Automated Storage & Retrieval System

A computerized information storage and retrieval system called Automation for Storage and Retrieval of Information (AFSARI) has been developed at the Bhabha Atomic Research Center (BARC), Bombay. The database contains bibliographical information of the library holdings. Programs have been written in COBOL language for the Honeywell 400 computer at the BARC computer facility for SDI service and for generating two current awareness lists : Bibliography of Current Reports and List of Additions. Several types of indexes including personal author index, descriptor index and report number index are also provided. The database also provides input to the International Nuclear Information System.

Computerised Selective Dissemination of Information

An experimental and pilot project on a computer-based SDI service using COBOL software was developed at the DRTC, Bangalore, and the actual studies were carried out at the Indian Institute of Science, Biochemistry Department and at the Bharat Heavy Electricals complex. The user interest profiles were prepared in consultation with the actual users and consisted of subject statements, keywords, author names, journal titles, and key references. The database for the pilot project consisted of full bibliographic data on articles drawn from 165 selected periodicals; other documents such as technical reports and these were also included. The Thesaurus of Engineering and Scientific Terms (TEST) and Medical Subject Headings (MeSH) were used for the purpose of vocabulary control in describing the document profiles.

INSDOC has successfully implemented an experimental SDI project based on CAN/SDI software with Unesco (UNISIST) assistance at the Indian Institute of Technology, Madras. At present, SDI service is being made available from Chemical Abstracts Condensates database to about 150 users, some of whom are in neighbouring countries. Other databases are expected to be added in the near future.

The SDI service operational at the BARC, Bombay, is based on its AFSARI system described earlier, and serves some 75 profiles representing "group" requirements for information (rather than "personal" information requirements). The service is now limited to report literature received at the depository library. The. output tape received from the International Nuclear Information System has not been used for SDI or other purposes at BARC for want of a compatible computer.

Future of SDI

Application of computers to library and information work influenced by several factors such as the size and rate of growth of library collections, the demand for expeditions information retrieval and dissemination services in libraries, the availability of trained personnel and financial resources for implementing and operating computerized systems, and the general level of "information infrastructure" obtaining in the country. A few institutes of research and higher education such as the Bhabha Atomic Research Center and the Institutes of Technology have attempted to computerize their library and information related activities to a limited extent. There is demand from the clientele in these institutes for expeditious, comprehensive and selective access to information. These institutes are also endowed with adequate resources in terms of strong library collections, trained personnel and computer facilities. In most other libraries, the demand for services and the resources available are not adequate to warrant the use of computers.

NISSAT

At the national level, however, the picture that is now emerging is entirely different. There is growing realization on the part of national planning and executive agencies of the pervasive and inevitable role of computers in all vital sectors of national endeavor including science and technology, industry, national defense, and education. The Electronics Commission, constituted in 1971, is responsible for developing a national policy, plans and goals for the electronics industry as a whole. Priority for computerization is given to applications that are of national significance (e.g. defense and export-oriented industries) and those "development-catalyzing" applications that are vital to the economic development of the country. These include: Agricultural information systems, management decision information systems, research and development, and industrial applications.

The Corporation has introduced three computer mainframes for small to medium class applications. These computers can handle real-time data acquisition and control applications, and are fully supported by both general purpose and special purpose peripheral equipment, interface electronics, and total system software packages for data processing and control applications.

The Electronics Center has also proposed a National Informatics Center to plan, develop and coordinate information-related projects and activities at a national level. The National Information System for Science and Technology (NISSAT) has envisaged the use of computer facilities for the bibliographic information processing, including provision of SDI service based on international bibliographic databases. A National Center for Software Development and Computing Techniques has also been set up at the Tata Institute of Fundamental Research to undertake developmental work in the following areas:

(1) Interactive computing and graphic techniques;

(2) Advanced programming;

(3) Basic software development techniques ;

(4) Operating system design ; and

(5) Remote use of computers and networking.

India is now on the threshold of online information retrieval era. A demonstration of online access to databases was organized at the Tata Institute of Fundamental Research Institute, Bombay, during September 20-25, 1976, using the RECON system of ESRIN (European Space Agency-European Space Research Information). The demonstration was organized by the Department of Science and Technology in collaboration with the Post and Telegraphs Department, Overseas Communication Service, Tata Institute of Fundamental Research, INSDOC, ESA/ESRIN, with assistance from Unesco-UNISIST. The objective of this project—the first of its kind to be organized in India-was to demonstrate to scientists, engineers, technologists, medical personnel and information specialists the application of computer and communication technologies for providing instant and interactive access to bibliographic information from remotely located databases. During the six-day demonstration, attended by some 1,500 scientists from all over the country, over 500 questions were searched in an online mode.

Successful implementation of the afore-mentioned national level plans calls for the development of qualified manpower to assess information needs and to participate in the tasks of designing, implementing and operating computer-based information systems. The Indian Institutes of Technology and some universities are offering courses in computer science, management information systems, and automation and control. These programs are not specifically geared to library and information applications. Some universities (e.g. the Delhi University) have begun master's degree programs in information science. INSDOC and DRTC have introduced computerized information storage and retrieval systems in their training programs.

20

Future of Automated Libraries

Overview

One major problem which arises when reliance is placed on the published literature in this way is the twofold difficulty of distinguishing between projects that are planned for some unspecified future date and those which are actually operational at the time of writing, and of learning about automated projects which have ceased to function. It is only natural that projects should be widely publicized at their inception and that their demise should be concealed from the public gaze. But librarians as a body will learn as much from honest reports of failures and the reasons for them as they will from reports about automated systems that are planned or newly-implemented. The lack of such a literature about failures is keenly felt, especially in the present context.

A second major purpose of this chapter is that it should provide for comment on the systems outlined in previous chapters. These systems are "ideal" and do not necessarily represent, any particular real-life operational systems. Although they are naturally based on real life, their purpose is to illustrate the principles embodied in real systems. In this chapter real systems are mentioned and the idealized systems of previous chapters are thrown into clearer relief by comparison with them.

Ordering Systems

The University Library in Newcastle-upon-Tyne has been operating a computer-aided ordering system since April 1966. The introduction of this system was facilitated in that it makes use of a number of programs already in existence as part of the Newcastle file-handling system. This is a suite of programs written for the English Electric KDF9 computer to facilitate the handling of structured data of the kind found in bibliographical applications. It is interesting to note that Newcastle University library report a small saving in staff time compared with the previous order system which used edge-notched cards. If computer time were charged to the library, however, the automated system would be considerably more expensive.

An ordering system which differs somewhat from these is operational in the Nassau Library system, New York. This is part of a data-processing service to fifty co-operating libraries in Nassau County, using a UNIVAC 1004 computer. For new books which are included in the Virginia Kirkus Service pre-punched cards are distributed, one for each title, giving the usual bibliographical information. To order one of these books all that a library has to do is to return the appropriate punched card to the data-processing centre indicating the number of copies needed. This is an interesting example of one way in which cooperation between libraries can make for simpler automated systems, save time, and reduce costs.

At the University of Maryland an acquisitions system is in operation utilizing punched-card equipment only. Orders and auxiliary listings of outstanding orders, receipts, and fund reports are made using an IBM 407 accounting machine. "On order" cards are filed manually in the public card catalogue and pre-cataloguing is carried out whenever complete Library of Congress cataloguing data is available.

A unique computer-aided system for ordering replacement copies of standard books is now operating in Toronto. Public librarians there have selected a standard list of about 2500 titles, all of which are available in paperback editions. Given information on the quality rating of publishers' editions, the computer prepares monthly lists of replacement orders which enable each branch library to have in stock a determined number of copies of all the standard titles, all in good condition. A number of library systems in the Toronto area are cooperating in this scheme which, because of its size, enables substantial discounts to be obtained.

A number of other libraries have reported automated acquisitions systems to be in operation. At the library of the University of Michigan a disc memory store is used in the computer processing of order records, while at the Redstone Scientific Information Center a system christened ALPHA (Automatic Literature, Processing, Handling, and Analysis) utilizes an IBM 632 electronic typing calculator for keypunching the original order records. The library of Washington University School of Medicine are also using a disc file and hope soon to develop on-line interrogation techniques using visual display consoles.

Circulation System

A typical computer-aided circulation system is now operational at the University of Southampton. It is being implemented in four stages of increasing sophistication the first of which commenced operation in October 1966 and the second in November 1967. The first stage, as a by-product of its operation, produces a book card for each book that is circulated, thus building up an "active" collection of books with book cards ready for automatic input of charging data during the second stage of the system. The final two stages provide for on-line interrogation and updating of the loans file.

The price which has to be paid for this gradual method of building up an active collection is the heavy work load involved with the first stage. Borrowers fill in slips for each book they borrow and reserve and data-processing staff keypunch one card for each of these transactions and also one card for each book that is returned. The alternative is a crash programme to prepare a book card for every volume in the library and this was in fact done at Texas A & M University using student labour. The advantage of such a crash programme is that the circulation system can employ automatic collection of charging data right from the very beginning, and that there will be no need to cater for books being circulated without cards.

Trueswell has shown that for a university technical library where it is the newest books that circulate most, it is more economical to prepare book cards for books on loan during the loan period than to carry out a crash programme for the entire collection. And if all new acquisitions are supplied with book cards at the technical processing stage, possibly as a by-product of an automated order system, then in time only a small percentage of books will be presented for circulation without book cards. However, in a public lending library where a high percentage of the stock is circulated and books have a long "half-life", a crash programme may be appropriate.

Ruecking has made a mathematical analysis of future circulation growth at Rice University in order to make a more accurate comparison between different methods of circulation control. As circulation increases and as files grow, linear relationships do not necessarily hold, so that it is necessary to include the cumulative costs of a system when evaluating it. His calculations show that over a 6-year period the total cumulative cost of a computerized system would be about half the cumulative cost of any other system.

A number of libraries in the United States have now adopted circulation control systems based on either the IBM 357 or 1030 data-collection units, accepting data from eighty-column punched book cards and readers' plastic badge cards. Among these are Southern Illinois University, Florida Atlantic University, Lehigh University, Oak Ridge National Laboratory, and the University of Missouri.

An unusual system operates at Johns Hopkins University which represents one solution to the slow charging speeds which are associated with computer-aided circulation control. The price paid is an extra operation in the circulation procedure. Charge and discharge data is captured on microfilm by photographing the reader's identification card and the spines of up to twelve or fifteen books being borrowed. After developing the film the data is keypunched and processed by the computer in the normal way.

In Germany, two university libraries, Bochum and the Technical University of Berlin, have implemented automated circulation control systems using book cards edge-punched with paper-tape codes for automatic collection of charging data. A full report has recently been published on the experiences gained from the Bochum system.

Circulation System With Punched Card

Circulation control systems using punched-card machines have not yet been displaced by computer-based systems. One has recently been installed in the Atomic Weapons Research Establishment at Alderaston. It makes use of the card duplicating facility of an IBM 026 printing card punch to create three transaction cards for each loan from punched book and reader cards. One card is filed manually in the issues file and the other two are used by a computer to apply various controls to the system; to test for overdue books, for example. Another system has been installed in the Widener Library of Harvard University. Eighty-column cards are filled in by borrowers and then keypunched for processing. A computer is used only for printing letters recalling overdue books.

Judging from the experience of the University of Hawaii it would be foolish to assume that computer-based circulation systems are the only ones worth introducing in this modern age. The best system for each individual library can only be arrived at after rigorous systems work and careful costing.

Accessioning System

Many libraries have produced lists of their periodicals holdings by computer or punched-card methods and taken advantage of the opportunities thus afforded for distributing the list widely and updating it easily and frequently. In Britain the University of Liverpool published a Finding List of Scientific Medical and Technical Periodicals in 1966, while at Loughborough University of Technology plans have reached an advanced stage for producing a novel holdings list, Coden are being used as brief unique identifiers for titles and will enable cross references to be created by the machine. Subject terms will be assigned to each title in order to prepare a subject index to the list.

A union list of periodicals held in Institute of Education libraries in Britain was also published in 1966. It was produced with the aid of some programs of the Newcastle file handling system. Experiments are in hand to print new editions of this union list by computer typesetting techniques being developed by the University of Newcastle-upon-Tyne computer typesetting project.

Periodical Listing

The Atomic Energy Research Establishment at Harwell produced printed list of its periodicals holdings by punched-card techniques in 1960. The main library at Harwell is responsible for purchasing periodicals for its own collections as well as for those of twenty-two divisional libraries. The use of mechanized methods for compiling the list made it a comparatively simple job to supply each library within the system with a frequently updated union list of periodicals.

The most important British union list of serials produced by mechanical means is, of course, the new BUCOP. Input is from punched cards and processing is done by IBM computer. In the case of a widely used list such as this it becomes important that computer typesetting techniques should be introduced quickly, even though the present frequently updated list is an immense improvement on the older ones.

Holdings lists have also been produced by punched-card methods in the National Research Council Library, Ottawa, and the libraries at Massachusetts Institute of Technology.

Semi-automated serials check-in systems have a number of attractive features and have been adopted by several libraries. They can be regarded as an intermediate stage between systems producing a list of holdings and fully automated systems embracing accounting, checking in, and binding routines for periodicals. For libraries which cannot afford to develop a fully automated system directly they are a useful stepping-stone whereby the final goal can be approached by degrees.

In Britain a computer-produced checking-in list has been developed at the City University. Periodical parts expected to arrive during the coming month are listed on a line printer. As the parts are received in the library they are ticked off on this list, making it a simple matter to inform library users about the arrival or non-arrival of a particular journal issue. This printed checking-in list gives full titles of journals, unlike systems which punch an eighty-column card for each expected part, where titles have to be abbreviated. The system is capable of conversion to a fully automated one, which would require only a minimum amount of keypunching to cater for parts which do not behave as expected.

Another semi-automated system has been installed at the Louisville School of Medicine, Louisville, Kentucky. Using only punched-card equipment, check-in cards are prepared for each expected title. These require the manual addition of volume number, part number, and date of receipt to complete the full bibliographical data for each part.

A number of libraries in the United States have reported the installation of fully automated computerized systems. Of these, the -most notable are at the University of California, San Diego, Washington University School of Medicine, Florida Atlantic University, and Purdue University, and in the Library of the U.S. Atomic Energy Commission, Washington, D. C.

Computerise Bibliographies & Catalogues

The very simplest level at which entries for bibliographies and catalogues can be prepared by automated methods is that involving the use of a paper-tape typewriter or the IBM Document Writer. These machines are used widely in libraries nowadays and their routine application is seldom reported in the literature. Two useful articles which explain how they have been used in particular libraries are those by Wilson and Bernstein. The way the IBM 870 Document Writer can be used to produce catalogue card sets and other listings is outlined in detail in an IBM report.

Conflicting reports have been published on the relative costs of producing catalogue cards by tape typewriter and by other techniques. Mackenzie shows the tape typewriter to be about 75 per cent as costly as either a stencil duplicator or a small offset litho machine. Moore, on the other hand, finds the reverse to be true-duplicating methods work out to be approximately 75 per cent as costly as tape typewriters. The cause of these divergent results is to be found in the relative amounts of clerical time stated to be required by the two methods. Mackenzie bases his calculations on the tape typewriter requiring only half the operator time that the duplicators require, whereas Moore's figures show that the duplicating method requires only five-eighths the operator time of the tape typewriter.

Methods of Preparing Catalogue Card

An interesting variation on these methods has been reported by Fasana et al. Catalogue records are prepared in machine-readable form and in a special machine-interpretable natural format using a nape typewriter. Working from the tape punched by the tape typewriter, a special digital machine-the Itek Crossfiler-prepares a second tape which contains, in machineable form, multiple formatted catalogue entries. Running this second tape through a tape typewriter produces the required card set directly. Briefly, this technique obviates the need to use a program tape when added entries are being typed and makes for greater flexibility in the production of added entries of different kinds.

Dewey gives a brief historical survey of the earliest catalogues produced by punched-card methods and records that the first non-experimental catalogue of books was made in 1951 for the branch libraries of King County (Washington) Public Library System. More widely known are the book catalogues of Los Angeles County Public Library, first introduced in 1953. Before that date only 26 of the system's 114 service outlets had card catalogues, while the introduction of book catalogues enabled each branch to have a union catalogue of the whole library system. Geller discusses the effect these catalogues had on the public service aspects of the Los Angeles Library System, concluding: "Our printed book catalogue was a child of necessity that has passed all the expectations of its fond adoptive 'parent.'"

A book catalogue produced by punched-card methods was introduced to the science and engineering libraries of the University of Rochester in 1962. This short-title catalogue, now made using an IBM 7094 computer, is designed as a supplement to the libraries' regular card catalogues and each entry is accordingly limited to one line only. In the latest editions of this catalogue refinements have been made to the sort programs. Abbreviations are filed as if they were spelled out in full and names which have prefixes such as de, le, ann, aon, etc., separated from the main name, are interfiled with names where the prefixes are not separated.

Computerize Catalogue in USA's University

In the North American libraries that have made book catalogues by computer are Stanford University Library, where the decision to automate was based on a thorough comparative cost analysis, Florida Atlantic University, where the original intention was that the catalogue should also be searchable by machine and Toronto University Library, which prepared a book catalogue of the combined holdings of five new university libraries in the province of Ontario the ONULP project.

At Harvard University Library a project is under way to convert the entire shelf list to machine-readable form. In that a shelf list is a classified sequence of bibliographic records, the whole job can conveniently be split into small units and one main class keypunched at a time. The first Harvard class, the Crusades, was completed in May 1965. As with the short title catalogue at the University of Rochester, these printed shelf lists, invaluable as they are, can only be regarded as supplements to the main card catalogue where full bibliographic details are available. De Gennaro has recently developed this class-wise conversion technique into a proposal for creating a national union catalogue in machineable form for the United States. Each class of the Library of Congress shelf list would be converted and machine printouts compared with the holdings of other large research libraries. They would add to the machineable records their own locational symbols and titles held only by them, and could print their own book catalogues by selective listing of the master tapes.

The medical libraries of Yale University and Columbia University are co-operating in a project which will eventually provide them with a common pool of books and journals the catalogue of which will be in machineable form and accessible through remote on-line consoles. Kilgour has described programs to produce printed catalogue cards as the first stage in this ambitious project. The programs were written in a symbolic-assembly language to take fullest advantage of the potential of a small computer-a two-tape 4K IBM. In another paper Kilgour outlines the advantages to be gained from writing programs in such a machine-orientated language as compared with a higher-level language such as COBOL, which was proposed by Culbertson as a standard language to be used for library data processing.

An unusual computer-produced catalogue on microfilm has been operational in the Technical Information Center of Lockheed Missiles & Space Company since July 1966. Using a machine to compose directly from the computer onto microfilm is stated to reduce costs considerably. Access to the catalogue must be by means of a microfilm reader, but film kept in cartridges makes for simple handling and a Xerox Copyflo can be used to produce hard copy quickly and cheaply if this is wanted.

MARC

The Library of Congress project MARC has had a marked influence on libraries' plans for catalogue automation both in North America and in Britain. The MARC pilot project, in which cataloguing copy was distributed on an experimental basis to sixteen libraries, began in October 1966 and is still continuing. References 76 and 77 provide useful information about this first stage of the project. Bregzis describes how the University of Toronto Library (one of the sixteen) fitted the weekly tapes into their regular cataloguing routines.

At the time of writing, the Library of Congress is developing an improved format for the catalogue records on MARC tapes, designed to facilitate the communication of bibliographic data in machineable form. Cowards describes this new format and discusses the United Kingdom MARC service, which is hoped to be made available within the next few years. It will be firmly based on co-operation with the Library of Congress, especially as co-operation has already been established in regard to the actual data going into catalogue records as part of the Library of Congress Shared Cataloging Program. The introduction of standard book numbering to the British book trade has provided a convenient tag for identifying the records on the British MARC tapes and should reduce greatly the problems associated with matching catalogue records by computer. A possible file structure for the weekly magnetic tapes produced by the U.K. MARC service might be as follows: firstly, a main file consisting of a series of catalogue records in standard book number order; and secondly, a title index to the first part of the file. The index might also be produced in printed form along with a listing of the SBN's of records in the first part of the file.

In Britain the Library of the University of Essex has been preparing book lists by computer for over a year:' Using a format based on that of the Library of Congress MARC Pilot Project, this work has not yet produced entries for the Library's card catalogue, although this would be within the capabilities of the system. Rather, the computer's ability to produce special subject listings has been exploited, in addition to preparing routine lists of accessions.

The public library systems of the London Boroughs of Barnet, Camden, and Greenwich have had computer-produced book catalogues for nearly 3 years now. Using the services of a computer bureau and accepting severe limitations on the format and layout of entries, these libraries have been able, nevertheless, to improve their public services by supplying all branches with union catalogues, a virtual impossibility with a manual system.

At the Cambridge Philosophical Library a project has commenced to produce by computer a union catalogue of books in the many departmental libraries within the University of Cambridge. The entire shelf lists of a sample of these libraries are being converted into machineable form and a thorough investigation will be made into the problems of merging the separate catalogues by computer and producing a union catalogue of the combined holdings. In another connection Richmond has discussed some of the difficulties which arise when merging entries in the computerized catalogues at the University of Rochester. Unless entries referring to identical books really are truly identical the computer will include them both in the updated catalogue. On the other hand, if the matching is not strict there is the danger that the machine will fail to distinguish between differing editions of a book, for example.

In Germany, book-form catalogues are being produced by computer at the University of Bochum. This is a new university and in fact has no card catalogue at all.

Germany has also made an important contribution to computer-aided cataloguing methods by being the first country to produce its national bibliography by computer. Since 1 January 1966 the weekly lists of the Deutsche Bibliographie and all supplements and cumulations have been published under the new system. Typesetting is by means of a Linoquick machine, a normal line-casting machine which can be controlled by paper tape. The main advantage of this data-processing system became apparent with the first half-yearly cumulation, the Halbjahres-Yerzeichnis. Normally this job takes from 12 to 15 months, but it has now been reduced to 2½ months.

Development of Automated Library

Automated library service in the future can only be predicted by educated extrapolation of the developments that arc taking place in libraries today, bearing in mind other factors which will have an important bearing on libraries. Included among these will be an expected continuing exponential growth in population and the increasing importance of libraries in the developing countries. The expansion of knowledge shows no signs of abating, and libraries will also be faced with a continuing proliferation of disciplines, coupled with a trend towards inter-disciplinary study. The volume of publications will continue to grow but there should be an increasing recognition by central governments of the importance of libraries and their functions of bibliographic control and information dissemination. The consequence of this recognition will be greater financial support for library programmes.

Library buildings, systems for subject representation, forms of publications, and the reader services provided for the library's clientele. Co-operation between libraries at local, national, and international levels will increase in importance, but it must be flexible so as to ensure that individual, important local needs and preferences will not be sacrificed to larger, seemingly more important goals. Most important of all, perhaps, is the recognition that libraries serve as an intermediary in processes of communication between human beings. They are not ends in themselves and the fact that libraries must deal ultimately with people, not merely with inanimate documents and machines, obliges us to design systems which treat both readers and library staff with understanding and respect for their personal feelings and needs.

Role of Computer in Library

The computer has a central role to play in such future library systems. A reliable, competent, accurate, and cheap manipulator of library information it can bring to fruition many idealistic concepts about flexible library services. In that it has the capacity to free human beings from much of the repetitive labour that is a necessary concomitant to library work, it can also give us the opportunity to provide personal service to real people. The necessary prerequisite to the wise and proper use of computing machinery in libraries in the future is a body of wise and informed library managers now.

It is possible to distinguish two general directions in which computer-aided library services will develop. Printed lists prepared by computer processing of a basic corpus of bibliographic records will increase in number and in diversity, and facilities far on-line interrogation of files held in machine memories will become more widely available.

At the present moment computer-aided library systems almost invariably produce as their end product some sort of printed list for human consultation or scanning. In the future, then, we can expect to see more such lists prepared in circumstances where they can be justified either by reducing costs or increasing services. The lists will become cheaper to produce and their quality will improve.

At present, too, a number of experimental on-line library projects are either operational or under development. It is reasonable to suppose that these will be successful and will eventually find application in certain circumstances.

Housekeeping Activities

The major area of library housekeeping which librarians tend to regard as being suitable for on-line methods is circulation control. Although no system is operational yet, work is either in progress or under consideration at the University of California, San Diego and Los Angeles, and at Harwell and Belfast. A proposal for on-line accessioning of periodicals has come from the University of Lancaster, and a number of libraries are considering systems for on-line manipulation of cataloguing data. Assuming that it remains essential to make non-programmable alterations either to ordering data or catalogue data from a central agency before it can be added to a library's own catalogue file, then an on-line visual display console equipped with a keyboard and light pen would appear to be an attractive piece of hardware for doing this. All of these on-line systems, however, involve only minor modifications to existing patterns of library activity.

More far-reaching changes to present-day methods of library use appear to be implied in on-line systems for information retrieval and text processing. Those that come closest to everyday library operations involve the on-line interrogation of a file of bibliographic records. The University of Toronto is actively involved in this area and Bregzis has put forward proposals for a query language for an on-line catalogue. This enables a search to be directed in the first place to the names of authors, editors, etc., titles, class numbers, or coden. Secondary search of a body of records retrieved by one of the above terms can be by means of a subject term; publisher's name, date of publication, place of publication, language, or location. The details of the system have yet to be worked out, including the bibliographic record format to be used, but the body of records will be indexed in four ways corresponding to the four data categories by which primary access to the file may be obtained. Presumably, search statements can combine more than one term in logical relationship.

A project is also under way to create an on-line union catalogue for the public libraries of metropolitan Toronto! Here, in addition to the design of the machine system, difficulties have to be overcome in respect of differences of cataloguing practice between co-operating libraries. It is likely that this project will provide for only limited degrees of search complexity, and will handle only abbreviated bibliographic records in order to minimize he size of file required.

Massachusetts Institute of Technology which permits on-line searching of bibliographical records by various novel search strategies. Articles from twenty-one specially chosen physics journals are "indexed" for the system, but conventional subject indexing is not employed except in so far as it is made available in Physics Abstracts. Search strategies can be defined on the basis of journal titles, authors' names, and keywords in titles. Citation-orientated searching is also possible. For example, one can search for all papers which cite a chosen article or, alternatively, all papers that have a stated number of references in common with the chosen article. Kessler has introduced the concept of bibliographic coupling to describe the linkage formed between papers which have references in common. Two papers are said to be bibliographically coupled with coupling strength of one (two, three, etc.) when they have one (two, three, etc.) references in common. Kessler has found that groups of papers coupled in this way are quite similar to the groups made by a conventional subject index.

Computerize Indexing

Indexing by means of bibliographic coupling is likely to become more common in future than it has been in the past. Relying on the authors of papers for the intellectual effort which is required for a good index, it demands the use of new search strategies on the part of library users. The technique is particularly suitable for machine applications in that no intellectual effort is required to construct the index. The printed volumes of Science Citation Index are compiled on these principles and make it possible to experiment now with search strategies which will be appropriate with some future on-line information retrieval systems.

On-Line Library System

A detailed description of an imaginary on-line library system has been given by Licklider. Termed a "procognitive system" in that it exists for, or to serve, knowledge and learning, it replaces the codex and the card index of present-day libraries by direct-access computer memories containing the same information. Computer processors in the procognitive system are able, in an unspecified way, to organize and mull over the data in store, and also to search it. Access to the system is by means of visual display terminals equipped with light pens, which make the system reminiscent of Vannevar Bush's prophetic description of MEMEX in 1945.

An experimental approach to such a system has been described by Bobrow et al. A program named SYMBIONT enables a number of basic operations to be performed on textual matter. Once a document has been input to the system, 150-word "pages" of it can be displayed on the face of a console. Pages can be turned forwards and backwards, and selected passages of text can be named and stored for future reference. Searches can then be made using these names.

Project INTREX is another experiment in the same general direction. Begun in late 1965 it is a research programme whose main aim is to provide, by 1975, a solution to the problems of large libraries by means of on-line computing techniques similar to those of SYMBIONT and the procognitive system.

There is, of course, a dual problem here. Not only must some very sophisticated computer programs be developed, but they must be related to an understanding of language and of the way human beings interact with the body of knowledge which these systems plan to hold in computer memory. The fact is that we are woefully ignorant of the ways in which scholars approach the literature of their subject, or the reason why readers come into a library. To design on-line computer systems which perform limited file-searching functions may be to miss the real needs of most library users.

The automation of library operations can very readily be regarded as a way of escape from the pressing problems of everyday life in a library; ordering and cataloguing books, answering awkward reference questions, tracing lost books. Automation will certainly simplify many of these tasks, but it must be built upon a sure foundation of good library practice which, as far as possible, prevents problems from arising. Librarians best know what the problems are in cataloguing, acquisitions work, reader service, and circulation control, and it is important that their knowledge be brought fully to bear on the job of designing automated systems in the first place. Librarians must understand fully what automation can do in all areas from book ordering to natural-language text processing.

Bibliography

Artandi, S. Information Concepts and Their Utility. *Journal of the American Society for Information Science, 24,* 242-245.

Baird, J. C. Information Theory and Information Processing. *Information Processing & Management, 20* (3), 373-381.

Bates, M. J. Guest Editor, 50th Anniversary Issues. *Journal of the American Society for Information Science (JASIS), 50* (11 & 12), 958-1162.

Bates, M. J. Invisible Substrate of Information Science. *Journal of the American Society for Information Science (JASIS), 50* , 1043-1050.

Bates, M. J. Tour of Information Science through the Pages of *JASIS*. *Journal of the American Society for Information Science (JASIS), 50* , 975-993.

Belkin, N. J. Information Concepts for Information Science. *Journal of Documentation, 34,* 55-85.

Belkin, N. J., & Robertson, S. E. Information Science and the Phenomenon of Information. *Journal of the American Society for Information Science, 27* , 197-204.

Beniger, J. R. Information and Communication: The New Convergence. *Communication Research, 15* (2), 198-218.

Boyce, B. R., & Kraft, D. H. Principles and Theories in Information Science. *Annual Review of Information Science and Technology (ARIST), 20* , 153-175.

Derr, R. L. Concept of Information in Ordinary Discourse. *Information Processing & Management, 21* (6), 489-499.

Dervin, B. Useful Theory for Librarianship: Communication, not Information. *Drexel Library Quarterly, 13* , 16-32.

Dolby, J. L. Data as Information. *Information Processing & Management, 20* (3), 407-415.

Ellis, D. Physical and Cognitive Paradigms in Information Retrieval Research. *Journal of Documentation, 48* (1), 45-64.

Elman, S. A. Humanization of Information Science. *Special Libraries, 67* , 421-427.

Fairthorne, R. A. Morphology of 'Information Flow'. *Journal of the Association for Computing Machinery, 14,* 710-719.

Farradane, J. Nature of Information. *Journal of Information Science, 1,* 13-17.

Gordon, D. B., & Sager, N. Method of Measuring Information in Language, Applied to Medical Texts. *Information Processing & Management, 21* (4), 269-289.

Green, R. Profession's Models of Information: A Cognitive Linguistic Analysis. *Journal of Documentation, 47* (2), 130-148.

Green, R. T., & Courtis, M. C. Information Theory and Figure Perception: The Metaphor that Failed. *Acta Psychologica, 25,* 12-36.

Hayes, R. M. Measurement of Information and Communication [MS] (pp. C1-C22).

Hjørland, B. Library and Information Science: Practice, Theory, and Philosophical Basis. *Information Processing and Management, 36* (3), 501-531.

Hjørland, B. Theory and Metatheory of Information Science: A New Interpretation. *Journal of Documentation, 54* (5), 606-621.

Hoffman, E. Defining Information: An Analysis of the Information Content of Documents. *Information Processing and Management, 16,* 291-304.

Houser, L. Documents: The Domain of Library and Information Science. *Library & Information Science Research, 8* , 163-188.

Ingwersen, P. Information and Information Science in Context. *Libri,* 42 (2), 99-135.

Kreither, H., & Kreither, S., *Cognitive Orientation and Behavior*. New York: Springer.

Leide, J. E. Emmorphosis: Information as Process. *Canadian Journal of Information Science, 6,* 35-37.

Leupolt, M. Some Considerations on the Nature of Information. *International Forum on Information and Documentation, 3* (3), 29-34.

Levi, I. Information and Ignorance. *Information Processing & Management, 20* (3), 355-362.

Levine, M. M. Informative Act and Its Aftermath: Toward a Predictive Science of Information. *Journal of the American Society for Information Science, 28*, 101-106.

Mackay, D. M. Information and Prediction in Human Sciences. In S. Dockyx & P. Bernays (Eds.), *Information and Prediction in Science.* New York: Academic Press.

Meadow, C. T., & Yuan, W. Measuring the Impact of Information: Defining the Concepts. *Information Processing and Management, 33* (6), 697-714.

Molholt, P. Nature of Information and Its Influence on Libraries. *Special Libraries, 75* (3), 347-251.

Oldman, C. *Scientism and Academic Librarianship.* Paper presented at the Information and Society: A Collection of Papers Presented at Meetings of the B.S.A. Libraries and Information Study Group, School of Librarianship, Leeds Polytechnic.

Ong, W. J. Literacy and Orality in Our Times. *Journal of Communication* , 197-204.

Otten, K. W. Basis for A Science of Information. In A. Debons, ed. (Ed.), *Information Science: Search for Identity.* New York: Marcel Dekker.

Paisley, W. *Information Science as a Multidiscipline: Twenty Questions and a Few Answers.* Paper presented at the Conference: Information: Relations With Other Disciplines, Chicago, January 14-16.

Pearson, C., & Slamecka. Semiotics Foundations of Information Science, I. Theory of Sign Structure. *Foundations, FIS-2*, 7-19.

Pratt, A. D. Informaton of the Image: A Model of the Communications Process. *Libri*. 27, 204-220.

Roberts, N. Social Considerations Towards a Definition of Information Science. *Journal of Documentation, 32*, 249-257.

Rudd, D. Do We Really Need World III? Information Science With or Without Popper. *Journal of Information Science, 8*, 99-105.

Schreider, Y. A. On the Semantic Charateristics of Information. *Information Storage and Retrieval, 2,* 221-233.

Shannon, C. E., & Weaver, W. Mathematical Theory of Communication, *Mathematical Theory of Communication* (pp. 3-19). Urbana, Ill.: University of Illinois Press.

Tenner, E. Impending Information Implosion. *Harvard Magazine,* 31-34.

Thompson, F. B. Organization is the Information. *American Documentation, 19,* 305-308.

Weaver, W. Recent Contributions to the Mathematical Theory of Communication. In C. E. Shannon (Ed.), *Mathematical Theory of Communication.*

Wersig, G., & Neveling, U. Phenomena of Interest to Information Science. *The Information Scientist, 9* (4), 127-140.

Wyatt, H. V. When does information become knowledge? *Nature, 235,* 86-89.

Ziman, J. M. Information, Communication, Knowledge. *Nature, 224,* 318-324.

INDEX